ONTENTS

A GUIDE TO

ROLL OF THUNDER, HEAR MY CRY

STEVE EDDY
WITH TONY BUZAN

Hodder & Stoughton

Cover photograph ©: Corbis UK Ltd
Mind Maps: Philip Chambers
Illustrations: Karen Donnelly

ISBN 0 340 75323 4

First published 1999
Impression number   10 9 8 7 6 5 4
Year   2003

The 'Teach Yourself' name and logo are registered trade marks of
Hodder & Stoughton Ltd.

Typeset by Transet Limited, Coventry, England.
Printed in Great Britain for Hodder & Stoughton Educational, a division of
Hodder Headline Plc, 338 Euston Road, London NW1 3BH by Cox and Wyman Ltd,
Reading, Berks.

There are five important things you must know about your brain and memory to revolutionize the way you study:

- ◆ how your memory ('recall') works *while* you are learning
- ◆ how your memory works *after* you have finished learning
- ◆ how to use Mind Maps – a special technique for helping you with all aspects of your studies
- ◆ how to increase your reading speed
- ◆ how to prepare for tests and exams.

Recall during learning
– THE NEED FOR BREAKS

When you are studying, your memory can concentrate, understand and remember well for between 20 and 45 minutes at a time. Then it needs a break. If you carry on for longer than this without a break your memory starts to break down. If you study for hours non-stop, you will remember only a small fraction of what you have been trying to learn, and you will have wasted hours of valuable time.

So, ideally, *study for less than an hour*, then take a five to ten minute break. During the break listen to music, go for a walk, do some exercise, or just daydream. (Daydreaming is a necessary brain-power booster – geniuses do it regularly.) During the break your brain will be sorting out what it has been learning, and you will go back to your books with the new information safely stored and organized in your memory banks. We recommend breaks at regular intervals as you work through the Literature Guides. Make sure you take them!

Recall after learning
– THE WAVES OF YOUR MEMORY

What do you think begins to happen to your memory straight after you have finished learning something? Does it immediately start forgetting? No! Your brain actually *increases* its power and carries on remembering. For a short time after your study session, your brain integrates the information, making a more complete picture of everything it has just learnt. Only then does the rapid decline in memory begin, and as much as 80 per cent of what you have learnt can be forgotten in a day.

However, if you catch the top of the wave of your memory, and briefly review (look back over) what you have been studying at the correct time, the memory is stamped in far more strongly, and stays at the crest of the wave for a much longer time. To maximize your brain's power to remember, take a few minutes and use a Mind Map to review what you have learnt at the end of a day. Then review it at the end of a week, again at the end of a month, and finally a week before your test or exam. That way you'll ride your memory wave all the way there – and beyond!

The Mind Map ®
– A PICTURE OF THE WAY YOU THINK

Do you like taking notes? More importantly, do you like having to go back over and learn them before tests or exams? Most students I know certainly do not! And how do you take your notes? Most people take notes on lined paper, using blue or black ink. The result, visually, is boring! And what does *your* brain do when it is bored? It turns off, tunes out, and goes to sleep! Add a dash of colour, rhythm, imagination, and the whole note-taking process becomes much more fun, uses more of your brain's abilities, and improves your recall and understanding.

A Mind Map mirrors the way your brain works. It can be used for note-taking from books or in class, for reviewing what you have just studied, and for essay planning for coursework and in tests or exams. It uses all your memory's natural techniques to build up your rapidly growing 'memory muscle'.

You will find Mind Maps throughout this book. Study them, add some colour, personalize them, and then have a go at drawing your own – you'll remember them far better! Stick them in your files and on your walls for a quick-and-easy review of the topic.

HOW TO DRAW A MIND MAP

1 Start in the middle of the page. This gives your brain the maximum room for its thoughts.
2 Always start by drawing a small picture or symbol. Why? Because a picture is worth a thousand words to your brain. And try to use at least three colours, as colour helps your memory even more.
3 Let your thoughts flow, and write or draw your ideas on coloured branching lines connected to your central image. These key symbols and words are the headings for your topic. Start like the Mind Map on page 8.
4 Then add facts and ideas by drawing more, smaller, branches on to the appropriate main branches, just like a tree.
5 Always print your word clearly on its line. Use only one word per line.
6 To link ideas and thoughts on different branches, use arrows, colours, underlining, and boxes (see page 17).

HOW TO READ A MIND MAP

1 Begin in the centre, the focus of your topic.
2 The words/images attached to the centre are like chapter headings; read them next.
3 Always read out from the centre, in every direction (even on the left-hand side, where you will have to read from right to left, instead of the usual left to right).

USING MIND MAPS

Mind Maps are a versatile tool – use them for taking notes in class or from books, for solving problems, for brainstorming with friends, and for reviewing and working for tests or exams – their uses are endless! You will find them invaluable for planning essays for coursework and exams. Number your main branches in the order in which you want to use them and off you go – the main headings for your essay are done and all your ideas are logically organized!

Super speed reading

It seems incredible, but it's been proved – the faster you read, the more you understand and remember! So here are some tips to help you to practise reading faster – you'll cover the ground more quickly, remember more, and have more time left for both work and play.

◆ First read the whole text (whether it's a lengthy book or an exam or test paper) very quickly, to give your brain an overall idea of what's ahead and get it working. (It's like sending out a scout to look at the territory you have to cover – it's much easier when you know what to expect!) Then read the text again for more detailed information.
◆ Have the text a reasonable distance away from your eyes. In this way your eye/brain system will be able to see more at a glance, and will naturally begin to read faster.
◆ Take in groups of words at a time. Rather than reading 'slowly and carefully' read faster, more enthusiastically.
◆ Take in phrases rather than single words while you read.
◆ Use a guide. Your eyes are designed to follow movement, so a thin pencil underneath the lines you are reading, moved smoothly along, will 'pull' your eyes to faster speeds.

Preparing for tests and exams

◆ Review your work systematically. Cram at the start of your course, not the end, and avoid 'exam panic'!
◆ Use Mind Maps throughout your course, and build a Master Mind Map for each subject – a giant Mind Map that summarizes everything you know about the subject.
◆ Use memory techniques such as mnemonics (verses or systems for remembering things like dates and events).
◆ Get together with one or two friends to study, compare Mind Maps, and discuss topics.

AND FINALLY...

Have *fun* while you learn – it has been shown that students who make their studies enjoyable understand and remember everything better and get the highest grades. I wish you and your brain every success! ⌐(Tony Buzan)

HOW TO USE THIS GUIDE

This guide assumes that you have already read *Roll of Thunder*, although you could read 'Background' and 'The story of *Roll of Thunder*' before that. It is best to use the guide alongside the novel. You could read the 'Who's who?' and 'Themes' sections without referring to the novel, but you will get more out of these sections if you do refer to it to check the points made in these sections, and especially when thinking about the questions designed to test your recall and help you think about the novel.

The different sections

The 'Commentary' section can be used in a number of ways. One way is to read a chapter or part of a chapter in the novel, and then read the commentary for that section. Keep on until you come to a test section, test yourself – then have a break! Alternatively, read the Commentary for a chapter, then read that chapter in the novel, then go back to the Commentary. Find out what works best for you.

'Topics for discussion and brainstorming' gives topics that could well feature in exams or provide the basis for coursework. It would be particularly useful for you to discuss them with friends, or brainstorm them using Mind Map techniques (see p. vii).

'How to get an "A" in English Literature' gives valuable advice on what to look for in a text, and what skills you need to develop in order to achieve your personal best.

'The exam essay' is a useful 'night before' reminder of how to tackle exam questions, though of course it will help you more if you also look at it much earlier in the year. 'Model answer' gives an example of an A-grade essay and the Mind Map and plan used to write it.

The questions

Whenever you come across a question in the guide with a star ✪ in front of it, think about it for a moment. You could even jot down a few words in rough to focus your mind. There is not usually a 'right' answer to these questions: it is important for you to develop your own opinions if you want to get an 'A'. The 'Test yourself' sections are designed to take you about 10–20 minutes each – which will be time well spent. Take a short break after each one.

Page numbers

Page references are to the Puffin Books, 1994 edition. If you have another edition, the page numbers may be slightly different, although the chapters will be the same.

KEY TO ICONS

Themes

A **theme** is an idea explored by an author. Whenever a theme is dealt with in the guide, the appropriate icon is used. This means you can find where a theme is mentioned just by flicking through the book. Go on – try it now!

Race

Justice

Family and community

Education

Growing up

Property

STYLE AND LANGUAGE

This heading and icon are used in the Commentary wherever there is a special section on the author's choice of words and **imagery**.

BACKGROUND

Roll of Thunder, Hear My Cry is set in Mississippi, one of the southern states of the United States. The story begins in 1933, but to understand the social and economic situation that is so much part of the story we must look back to the seventeenth century. This was when black Africans first came to North America as slaves. Over 35 million were shipped across the Atlantic, in appalling conditions. About 15 million survived the voyage.

The slave trade was officially made illegal in 1807, but by then the economy of the southern states of the United States depended on slave labour to work the tobacco, rice, sugar and cotton plantations. Added to this, the invention of the cotton gin – a machine that separated cotton fibres from seeds – had helped to create a boom in the cotton industry. Therefore slavery continued in the South.

After the American Civil War (1861–5), the slaves were freed and given equal civil and political rights. During Reconstruction (1865–77) the government tried to reunite the North and South, and to improve social conditions in the South. Government agencies helped former slaves to find shelter, work and lost relatives. However, when the occupying troops went home, the South began to return to its old ways. By 1900 several states, including Mississippi, had passed 'Jim Crow' laws taking equality away from black people and reinstating racial segregation.

In addition to this legal undermining of their rights, black people also had to contend with the physical attacks of the Ku Klux Klan. (Remember the spelling: Ku not Klu.) This was a white racist organization, formed in 1865 to terrorize and subdue black people. Members rode out by night wearing white hoods and robes, sometimes burning crosses for extra effect. Between 1865 and 1896 the Klan and other racists lynched over 10,000 blacks. Laws were passed against the Klan in 1871, but it was revived after the First World War, and was very active during the 1930s.

In October 1929 the Wall Street Crash occurred. Public confidence in investment plummeted, people panicked in the rush to sell shares, and share prices fell alarmingly. This started the Depression, a period when people were afraid to invest in business and industry, leading to low productivity and high unemployment.

The South, already poorer than the North, was badly hit by the Depression, especially when cotton prices fell. Sharecroppers like the Averys (see Commentary, p. 43), already on the breadline, became even worse off. At the same time racism increased – in both America and Europe (for example in Hitler's Germany), as people looked for scapegoats on whom to blame their problems. At the start of *Roll of Thunder, Hear My Cry* this is already happening, especially among poor whites like the Wallaces.

A lot of background is given in the novel itself. Read Chapter 4, p. 85, for Mr Turner's account of what it means to be a sharecropper, at the mercy of the landowner, and Chapter 6, pp. 106–7, for an explanation of how whites in the South came to see black people as being sub-human.

The author

Mildred Taylor was born in Mississippi. Her parents, like many black people before them, made the move to the North, and she grew up in Ohio. However, she continued to visit Mississippi with her parents, as well as hearing the family history from her father, to whom she dedicates the novel.

She has said that the real-life characters in her father's stories 'were graced with a simple dignity that elevated them from the ordinary to the heroic'. This heroic quality was something she found completely lacking in the official white accounts of black history. When she wrote the novel, one of her aims, therefore, was to portray the black heroes and heroines missing from the schoolbooks of her own childhood.

The Logans are a black family living in Mississippi. Returning to school after the summer, the Logan children are **mud-soaked** by the white students' bus. At school, when **Little Man** finds a **label** inside his book revealing that it is considered unfit for white children, he throws the book down. Cassie also rejects hers, and Miss **Crocker** beats them both. Mrs Logan explains their reason, and covers the offending labels.

Papa brings Mr **Morrison** to stay. John Berry, burned by the Wallaces, dies. The Logans **boycott** the Wallace **store** and forbid the children to go there.

When the school **bus** gives the children another mud-bath, they dig a hole in the road, into which the bus plunges. Later, Cassie is terrified when the **Ku Klux Klan** approach the house – but then drive away. The Logan children fear a Klan reprisal, until TJ reveals that they have tarred and feathered **Sam Tatum**. At school, **Stacey** gets blamed for TJ's **cheat notes**. Stacey fights TJ at the **Wallace store**, but is stopped by Mr **Morrison**, who persuades him to confess to visiting the store. **Mama** responds by taking the children to see Mr **Berry**, suffering from burns inflicted by the Wallaces. She encourages other families to avoid the store.

In **Strawberry**, TJ persuades Stacey and Cassie into the Barnett **store** – where Cassie is discriminated against by Barnett. Next she bumps into a white girl, **Lillian Jean Simms**, is pushed by Mr Simms, and is forced to **apologize**. Uncle **Hammer** comes home from Chicago and hears about it. He sets off to teach **Simms** a lesson – but Mr **Morrison** talks him out of it. Cassie complains to Mama about having to apologize, and receives a lesson in the history of racial prejudice. **Hammer** gives Stacey a new **coat**. Stacey is delighted, but **TJ teases** him about it. The Wallaces give way to Hammer's car, mistaking it for Granger's.

Stacey gives his **coat** to TJ. To teach Stacey a lesson, **Hammer** says TJ can **keep** it. **Papa** returns for **Christmas**. On Christmas

Eve, Mr Morrison tells how the Klan killed his parents. The children get books for Christmas. The **Averys** come for **dinner**, and **Jeremy** Simms brings presents. After Christmas Mr **Jamison** offers to back the **credit** of families **boycotting** the Wallace store. Several days later **Granger** tries to **pressurize** the Logans into dropping the boycott.

Cassie gains **Lillian Jean's** confidence and **beats her up** in the forest. Mrs Logan **fails TJ** for cheating in his final exams. Soon after, she is **fired** from her teaching job. Stacey discovers that TJ is partly to blame – **TJ** is **shunned**.

TJ is keeping bad company, and the Wallaces are threatening black families. Some stop **shopping** at **Vicksburg**. Papa, Mr Morrison and Stacey go there, and on the way back are **attacked** by the Wallaces. Papa is wounded and his leg is broken by the wagon – but Mr **Morrison** badly **injures** two of the Wallaces.

Money is short for the Logans. Mr Morrison goes out in the wagon with the children. **Kaleb Wallace** deliberately blocks the road with his **truck**, but Mr Morrison lifts it out of the way. The Logan finances worsen when the **bank** demands repayment of its loan. **Hammer** sells his **car** to help. At a community festival **TJ** turns up with two white boys, **RW** and **Melvin** Simms, hoping to impress people.

TJ comes to the Logan home badly **hurt**. He and the Simms brothers have robbed the **Barnett store**, leaving the Barnetts for dead. The brothers have beaten TJ for threatening to reveal their guilt. Stacey and the other children help **TJ home**. Soon white men arrive looking for TJ. The Averys are beaten. Mr **Jamison** struggles to stop a **lynching**, weakly backed by the sheriff.

Cassie and her younger brothers get home, and Papa goes to **save** TJ and protect Stacey. Mary pleads with him not to use his gun, so he starts a **fire** to divert attention from TJ. Blacks and whites are briefly **united** in extinguishing it, and TJ is taken into custody.

HOW MUCH CAN YOU REMEMBER?

Try to fill in the words missing from this summary without looking at the original. Feel free to use your own words if they have the same meaning.

The Logans are a black family living in Mississippi. Returning to school after the summer, the Logan children are _____ by the white students' bus. At school, when _____ _____ finds a _____ inside his book revealing that it is considered unfit for white children, he throws the book down. Cassie also rejects hers, and Miss _____ beats them both. Mrs Logan explains their reason, and covers the offending labels.

Papa brings Mr _____ to stay. John Berry, burned by the Wallaces, dies. The Logans _____ the Wallace _____ and forbid the children to go there.

When the school _____ gives the children another mud-bath, they dig a hole in the road, into which the bus plunges. Later, Cassie is terrified when the ___ ___ ___ approach the house – but then drive away. The Logan children fear a Klan reprisal, until TJ reveals that they have tarred and feathered _____ _____. At school, _____ gets blamed for TJ's _____ _____. Stacey fights TJ at the _____ _____, but is stopped by Mr _____, who persuades him to confess to visiting the store. _____ responds by taking the children to see Mr _____, suffering from burns inflicted by the Wallaces. She encourages other families to avoid the store.

In _____, TJ persuades Stacey and Cassie into the Barnett _____ – where Cassie is discriminated against by Barnett. Next she bumps into a white girl, _____ _____ _____, is pushed by Mr Simms, and is forced to _____. Uncle _____ comes home from Chicago and hears about it. He sets off to teach _____ a lesson – but Mr _____ talks him out of it. Cassie complains to Mama about having to apologize, and receives a lesson in the history of racial prejudice. _____ gives Stacey a new _____. Stacey is delighted, but _____ _____ him about it. The Wallaces give way to Hammer's car, mistaking it for Granger's.

Stacey gives his _____ to TJ. To teach Stacey a lesson, _____ says TJ can _____ it. _____

returns for _____. On Christmas Eve, Mr Morrison tells how the Klan killed his parents. The children get books for Christmas. The _____ come for _____, and _____ Simms brings presents. After Christmas Mr _____ offers to back the _____ of families _____ the Wallace store. Several days later _____ tries to _____ the Logans into dropping the boycott.

Cassie gains _____ _____ confidence and ___ ____ ___ in the forest. Mrs Logan _____ _____ for cheating in his final exams. Soon after, she is _____ from her teaching job. Stacey discovers that TJ is partly to blame – _____ is _____.

TJ is keeping bad company, and the Wallaces are threatening black families. Some stop _____ at _____. Papa, Mr Morrison and Stacey go there, and on the way back are _____ by the Wallaces. Papa is wounded and his leg is broken by the wagon – but Mr _____ badly _____ two of the Wallaces.

_____ is short for the Logans. Mr Morrison goes out in the wagon with the children. _____ _____ deliberately blocks the road with his _____, but Mr Morrison lifts it out of the way. The Logan finances worsen when the _____ demands repayment of its loan. _____ sells his _____ to help. At a community festival _____ turns up with two white boys, _____ and _____ Simms, hoping to impress people.

_____ comes to the Logan home badly _____. He and the Simms brothers have robbed the _____ _____, leaving the Barnetts for dead. The brothers have beaten TJ for threatening to reveal their guilt. Stacey and the other children help _____ _____. Soon white men arrive looking for TJ. The Averys are beaten. Mr _____ struggles to stop a _____, weakly backed by the sheriff.

Cassie and her younger brothers get home, and Papa goes to _____TJ and protect Stacey. Mary pleads with him not to use his gun, so he starts a _____ to divert attention from TJ. Blacks and whites are briefly _____ in extinguishing it, and TJ is taken into custody.

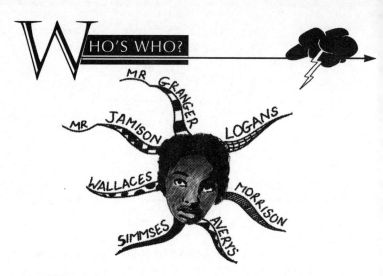

WHO'S WHO?

The Mini Mind Map above summarizes the characters in *Roll of Thunder, Hear My Cry*. Test yourself by looking at the full Mind Map on p. 17, and then copying the Mini Mind Map and trying to add to it from memory.

The Logans

The Logans are a black family. The adults share strong moral values, and they set a good example to the children. They support each other in times of trouble, for example when Mary Logan loses her job, and they have a sense of responsibility to the community. The adults take a pride and pleasure in the family land, and they teach the children its importance to the family's independence. The love and respect between them provides a secure emotional base for the children.

CASSIE

At nine years old, Cassie is already a forceful character. She has strong opinions, and at times expresses them without considering the consequences – for example when the store owner Barnett insults her she angrily informs him: *'I ain't nobody's little nigger! ... And you ought not be waiting on everybody 'fore you wait on us'* (p. 94). We see here, too, her stubborn refusal to tolerate the injustice of life in Mississippi. One way in which she develops in the novel is in learning to view this injustice in a more detached way, but without accepting it.

Cassie is an independent-minded girl. At school she dislikes taking part in class responses (p. 22), and is prepared to challenge the teacher when she rejects her textbook. In fact she dislikes school generally, and would rather be wandering the forest in her old clothes. Perhaps it is partly because of her independent spirit that she has no friends – other than her family. ✪ Why do you think it is?

We have seen Cassie's hot-headedness in the store incident. Papa tells her, *'... you got yourself a bad temper like your Uncle Hammer'* (p. 143). She is quick to defend herself – physically if necessary, assertive with classmates and impatiently dismissive of fools like TJ. She is also impulsive – even thoughtlessly so at times, as when she blurts outs a dismissal of Jeremy's present to the family (*'Nuts!'*). Mama scolds her: *'What have I told you about that mouth of yours?'* (p. 127).

Despite her impulsiveness, Cassie is able to plan her revenge on Lillian Jean and feign subservience to the white girl for a month so that she can eventually beat her up. Cassie is learning self-control – though she also learns that revenge is less satisfying if the victim fails to learn the desired lesson. ✪ Was it worth the effort and risk?

Closely related to Cassie's hot head is her warm heart. She adores her parents, longing for Papa to come home, and enjoying helping Mama to dress (p. 109). She also loves and respects Big Ma. She quickly warms to Mr Morrison, is excited to see Uncle Hammer and likes Mr Jamison. She can also be sensitive, understanding and compassionate. She sympathizes with Stacey when he blames himself for Papa's broken leg, and by the end of the novel she feels for TJ, even though she has never liked him.

STACEY

Twelve-year-old Stacey is almost a teenger and anxious to become a man. As the eldest of the Logan children – and especially with his father away on the railroad – he feels a responsibility for his brothers and sister, and for the family as a whole. Like his father, he thinks before acting, and is good at organizing others. We see both traits when he engineers the revenge on the school bus (Ch. 1). Equally, we see his burden of responsibility when the children think that the Ku Klux Klan are coming to get them.

Although Stacey looks before he leaps, he does not always make the right decision. In particular he allows TJ to get him into trouble. A prime example is when he gets fooled into giving his new coat to TJ (Chs 6–7). He takes bad advice from the slightly older boy – for example, on going into the Barnett store (Ch. 5), and he stops TJ cheating in an exam, but in the process gets the blame for TJ's *cheat notes*. His sense of honour will not let him reveal TJ's guilt, and he takes his punishment. Then he goes in pursuit of TJ, disobeying his parents by going to the Wallace store – for which he and the other children eventually receive a beating.

One positive outcome from this incident is what he learns from Mr Morrison about taking responsibility for his own actions. He also comes to respect Mr Morrison, whom he has up until now resented as a challenge to his position as 'man of the house' while his father is away.

When TJ gets Mama fired, Stacey has learnt that there are more effective ways to teach him a lesson than a fist-fight. However, although Stacey rejects TJ as a friend after this, he still has enough feeling for him to help TJ in his hour of need, after he and the Simms brothers have broken into the Barnett store. ✪ What do you feel about Stacey's decision to help?

CHRISTOPHER-JOHN

Cheerful seven-year-old Christopher-John is a gentle, sensitive boy whose plumpness suggests his softness of character. He hates bad feeling and avoids confrontations, *preferring to remain on good terms with everyone* (p. 2). He is less adventurous than the others, and tries to keep out of trouble. However, his reluctance to be left behind usually overrides this. The exception – showing his growing independence – is in the final chaper when Cassie and Little Man go to look at the fire damage (p. 213).

Although easy-going, there are things of which Christopher-John disapproves. One such thing is Cassie's apparently ingratiating behaviour towards Lillian Jean; another is when TJ gets Claude a beating. Christopher-John sympathizes with Claude then, and feels for him when he is hurt by the white mob in Chapter 11.

LITTLE MAN

Clayton Chester – usually known as Little Man (or even plain 'Man') is an independent six-year-old. Like his Uncle Hammer, he takes a pride in his appearance, and he hates dirtying his clothes. His independence and cleanliness are summed up on the first page: *'Y'all go ahead and get dirty if y'all wanna ... Me, I'm gonna stay clean.'*

Like Cassie, Little Man has a fighting spirit and is outraged by injustice – as when he is muddied and soaked by the school bus (Ch. 1). He also has quite a fiery temper, not just rejecting his school book, but stamping on it *madly* and refusing to pick it up (p. 25). On the other hand, when he gets a book for Christmas, he treasures it, repeatedly washing his hands for fear of spoiling it (p. 126).

MAMA – MARY

Mrs Logan – Mama – is a devoted mother and a teacher *'... born to teaching as the sun is born to shine'* (Papa, p. 152). In both roles she is strict but fair, her strictness springing from love and a desire to do what is best for the children. The first thing we hear about her is her willingness to administer physical punishment, and she even beats Stacey in front of the class when she catches him with TJ's *cheat notes.*

Some of her colleagues regard her as *too radical*, even as a *disrupting maverick*. She is certainly an intelligent and independent thinker, and while she is realistic about surviving the racial discrimination of the South, she works to undermine it. Her uncompromising nature is shown by the lesson in black history that she continues to teach in the presence of the racist school board members (p. 150). On the other hand she discourages Papa from courting danger, and does her best to prevent Hammer from challenging Simms.

11

PAPA – DAVID

At the start of the novel Papa is away working on the railroad. The fact that he is doing this is one key to his character. He is prepared to make sacrifices for the sake of his family, and to maintain the independence and relative security conferred by its land.

Whereas Hammer is hot-tempered and rushes into action, Papa is a thinker. He takes time to explain to Cassie the importance of the land, and she can go to him for advice – *for he always took time to think through any move he made.* He understands the value of self-respect, and teaches it to his children. He tells Cassie that there are *'... things you gotta take a stand on'*, but that it is important to consider what these things are, and what the consequences will be.

Although a disciplinarian who takes responsibilities seriously, Papa has a lighter side to him, as when he jokes affectionately with Mama about why she married him (p. 168).

BIG MA

Big Ma is David and Hammer's mother, a strong, hard-working woman who plays an important role in the household – and shares a bed with Cassie. She thinks wistfully about her late husband, Paul Edward, and remembers affectionately how he named the pond Caroline after her. She has a feeling for family history and worries about losing the land. She prays in times of trouble and anticipates meeting her husband in heaven.

Big Ma is not easily panicked. When danger threatens we see her quietly framed in the doorway with a shotgun. However, she is aware of the need to compromise in order to survive – which is why she makes Cassie apologize to Lillian Jean. Similarly she joins with her daughter-in-law in trying to prevent Hammer from getting himself killed.

UNCLE HAMMER

David's well-dressed, hot-headed younger brother Hammer works in the north, in Chicago, because there he can get *... a man's wage.* Perhaps, too, he knows that in Mississippi he would sooner or later get into trouble – as he almost does when he roars off into the night to pay Simms back for hurting Cassie.

Although he is impulsive, and talks bitterly about setting fire to the Wallace store, Hammer takes family responsibilities seriously. We see this when he gives Stacey a new coat and Stacey gives it to TJ. Hammer gives his nephew a withering *tongue-lashing*, and rules that TJ can keep the coat. Later, though proud of his luxurious car, he sells it to save the family land.

Mr Morrison

The most obvious thing about Mr Morrison is his size. He is over 7 feet (210 cm) tall (revealed in the sequel to *Roll of Thunder*), and immensely strong. His parents were born on farms where slaves were bred for strength. He has lost his railroad job after a fight with some white men, whom he has hurt *pretty bad*, and he inflicts serious damage on the Wallaces when they attack the Logans' wagon. His greatest feat of strength, however, is when he lifts the Wallaces' truck (Ch. 10).

Given Mr Morrison's strength – not to mention his staying up all night to guard the Logan house, it is may surprise you to find that he is 63 years old. (See pp. 121-3, and bear in mind the current date, p. 26.) ✪ Is this believable? Ask your grandparents!

Mr Morrison is a calm, quiet man who likes his privacy (p. 67). He does not speak much – his longest speech is about losing his parents (pp. 121–3), but he is thoughtful and has an inner strength to match his muscle-power. He can be cheerful, as when he sings with the children, and he is deeply appreciative of the Logans as his new family.

Mr Morrison is a mysterious character – we hear little about his past. However, his importance is evident in his link with the novel's title. His voice is like *low thunder*, and he sings a defiant blues song beginning *Roll of thunder/ hear my cry* (p. 194). ✪ What message do you think Mildred Taylor is conveying by this?

TJ Avery and family

TJ is the most important Avery in the novel. His well-intentioned but weak and overworked parents, and his long-suffering brother Claude, are only really significant in relation to him – although the nervous, sickly Joe Avery does also represent the poorest of black sharecroppers.

TJ is a cheerful, talkative boy with an easy charm. However, he is also devious and manipulative. His only worry seems to be failing his school exam, and he tries more than once to persuade Stacey to help him cheat. He is unscrupulous too, allowing both Claude and Stacey to get beatings rather than admit his own guilt.

Jealous of Stacey's coat, he cunningly persuades him to part with it and then boasts about owning it (Chs 6–7). He also shows a disregard for others – and perhaps a vengeful streak – when he gets Mrs Logan fired.

Despite his own slyness, TJ is extremely gullible. Memorize his boast about the Simms brothers: *'Everything I want they give me 'cause they really like me. I'm they best friend'* (p. 192). We also see here TJ's longing for the kind of showy possessions that his family will never have. This is tied up with his longing for attention, which Mary Logan points out (Ch. 9). His downfall is due to his dream of owning the pearl-handled pistol and the glamour that it represents, and his failure to realize how he is being used and led into danger.

Jeremy Simms and family

The Simms family are poor whites. Jeremy is a shy, stammering, dreamy boy who prefers the Logan children to his own family. He walks to school with them rather than go on the white school bus, although he gets beaten for it, and he joins them in the forest. At Christmas he risks rejection and punishment by taking presents to the Logans. He even offers to help the children build a tree-house like the one in which he sleeps. ❷ Do you respect his lack of racism, or think he's naive?

Lillian Jean Simms is a stuck-up girl so indoctrinated by the racism of her unpleasant father, Charlie Simms, that she cannot understand why Cassie tricks her. RW and Melvin are her older brothers. They manipulate and secretly mock TJ, beat him viciously, and then join the mob wanting to lynch him for the crime they committed.

The Wallaces

The Wallaces represent the worst kind of poor whites. They are violent racists who burn the Berrys, encourage black teenagers to run up debts for their parents by drinking and smoking at their store, and bitterly resent the Logans. In Chapter 11 they want to lynch TJ and *take care of* Mr Morrison and David Logan at the same time.

Mr Jamison

The only decent, rational, non-racist white man in the novel, Mr Jamison has an important role to play. Cassie likes him, and there is mutual respect between him and the Logans. He is courageous and idealistic enough to support the Logan-led boycott of the Wallace store. Yet he is neither naive nor patronizing. His long speech when he visits the Logans (pp. 134–5) shows his grasp of the situation. He is also bravely determined to save TJ from a lynching.

Mr Granger

Harlan Granger is a wealthy landowner. His family has been in the area for generations and he resents the Logans owning what was once Granger land. He is prepared to use underhand means to regain it if persuasion and veiled threats fail to work. When he 'inspects' Mary Logan's teaching, he displays his usual unpleasant irony, saying that she must be *'… some kind of smart … to know more than the fellow who wrote that book.'* Even when he says, in effect, that she's fired, he does it in the tone of a man who feels smug enough about his power to wield it with a cynical joke.

Although not openly violent, he is callous and exploitative. It is typical that he will not allow a lynching on his land, but does not oppose it taking place elsewhere.

Explore the characters

? Make up sentences describing the relationships between the characters paired below. Use the words given, if you wish. Find evidence for each sentence.

Stacey – TJ   Cassie – Stacey   Mr Jamison – Papa
Cassie – Papa

respects   adores   teaches   helps   obeys
exploits   punishes   tolerates

? Test yourself using the Mind Map opposite with the Mini version at the start of the section.

that's enough character exploration for now — explore something else for a while!

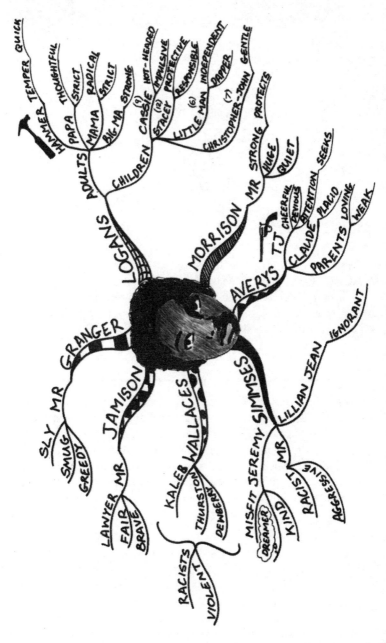

THEMES

A theme is an idea developed or explored throughout a work. The Mini Mind Map above shows the main themes of *Roll of Thunder, Hear My Cry*. Test yourself by copying the Mini Mind Map above, adding to it, and then comparing your results with the version on p. 23.

Race

Mississippi provided Mildred Taylor with a setting in which the issue of race would be ever-present. Race is the most important theme in the novel, and it relates to all the themes identified below – especially to justice, since Mississippi's racial prejudice creates an unjust society, in which the Wallaces can murder black men without being brought to court, and in which Mary Logan can lose her job because a white landowner wants her to.

Even where mutual respect exists, as between David Logan and Mr Jamison, there can be no friendship. Jeremy Simms likes the Logans, but they never let him become a real friend. When Stacey asks if it is wrong to like him, Papa tells him, *'That ain't wrong,'* but that *'... friendship between black and white don't mean that much 'cause it usually ain't on a equal basis.'* More bluntly, he adds that *'... white folks mean trouble,'* although he accepts that one day friendship may be possible (p. 130). Certainly that day has not come for TJ, whose association with whites ends in disaster.

Mildred Taylor explains the background to prejudice on pp. 106–7, through Mama. Significantly, Mr and Mrs Logan do not descend to hatred of whites, despite much provocation. The reason is that they understand the basis of prejudice – ignorance. ✪ How do you think the other black adults feel about whites?

Justice

Justice of a non-racial kind features in the way the Logan parents discipline their children, and in Mary Logan's strict punishment of students – even Stacey – suspected of cheating. However, as shown above, justice in this novel usually relates to race.

First there is the social injustice of the poverty of the black school compared with the white one, and of the black children walking to school while white students go by bus. Then there is the plight of the black sharecroppers obliged to remain in debt to landowners like Granger. They cannot choose where to shop, and if they query their bill they are likely to be tarred and feathered, like Sam Tatum.

We see justice in a second sense, on the personal level, when the Logans get their revenge on the white school bus driver and his passengers, and when Cassie gets her own back on Lillian Jean. ✪ Are these acts 'justice', or simply revenge?

Finally, there is the 'rule of law' – a mark of a civilized society – represented by Mr Jamison (J for Jamison and Justice!), who is quietly determined to see that TJ gets *true* justice rather than the violent mob's version of it.

Family and community

The author has commented that in writing *Roll of Thunder, Hear My Cry* she wanted:

> ... to show a family united in love and self-respect, and parents, strong and sensitive, attempting to guide their

children successfully, without harming their spirits, through the hazardous maze of living in a discriminatory society.

The Logans are the model against which other families in the novel are measured. For example, the Averys – poorer and with twice as many children – are well-intentioned but unable to control TJ. Joe Avery is physically weak, but in addition the parents lack the character or energy to keep TJ in line. Mr and Mrs Jamison are like David and Mary in that they discuss important decisions with each other.

The Wallaces, united in their violent racism, show another face of family life. Charlie Simms has successfully passed on his racism to his daughter, and his violence to his two elder sons, but has failed to indoctrinate the family misfit – Jeremy. Harlan Granger shows another negative side of family influence. His grandmother has filled him with *tales about the glory of the South before the war* (p. 126), which still fuel his obsession with regaining former Granger land.

Community in this novel is an extension of family. David and Mary Logan share a sense of responsibility towards their community, which is why they endanger themselves by leading the boycott. When TJ is in danger, David risks his life to help him, despite the fact that TJ has turned against the black community – first by getting Mary Logan fired, and then taking up with RW and Melvin.

Education

Education takes two forms in *Roll of Thunder*: formal and informal. The formal kind takes place in school. The novel begins with the Logan children on their way to school: Cassie is particularly reluctant. However, we hear that some black children – Moe Turner is one of them – undertake a three-and-a-half-hour walk to get to school.

Strangely, Mrs Logan never explains the importance of education. However, we do see her giving a lesson in black history and refusing to change it for Mr Granger, or to teach the lies printed in the textbook. We can, therefore, assume that one of her aims is to empower her students with the truth. The other reason for going to school is material and social advancement. Big Ma tells Little Man that one day he'll have more clothes, and perhaps a car – providing he sticks to his education (p. 42).

The informal kind of education is passed on from adult to child, usually one-to-one. Big Ma teaches Cassie about the history of the Logan land; Mama teaches her about slavery and how it gave rise to racial discrimination; and Papa teaches her about self-respect. ❍ Which kind of education seems more effective in the novel?

Growing up

Growing up is linked to education, but it involves learning from experience – often through suffering. Little Man grows up a little when told that there is no school bus for blacks. Cassie learns from her two encounters with racism in Strawberry (Ch. 5). And she has come a long way when, at the end of the novel, she cries for TJ and the land.

Stacey does more growing up than anyone else in the novel, learning lessons about responsibility for his own actions – with the help of Mr Morrison, and about friendship. He is unfortunate enough to have in TJ an unworthy, unreliable friend who is the 'right' colour, and in Jeremy someone who could make a better friend – except that he is the 'wrong' colour. ❍ What do you think Stacey learns from each?

Property

The first and most important form that property takes in *Roll of Thunder* is land ownership. In Chapter 1 Cassie recounts what Papa has told her about the land, and in Chapter 4 Big Ma tells her more. The Logans regard their land as their security, and take a pride in how the family acquired and kept it. But they also value it in a deeper sense. They all seem to find peace sitting in the forest.

Compare this with Granger's attitude. Land for him is a means of exploiting the sharecroppers, but also of boosting the family name and his own status – as if he will become a bigger man if he owns more land. His Packard car is also a status symbol, whereas Hammer's car symbolizes personal achievement. Hammer enjoys the car, but he values it less than his family.

Tied in closely with the land are the local economy and family finances. We hear that Granger pays a top rate of 50 cents a day to cotton pickers, and we learn how the sharecroppers are forced into dependence on the landowners. The Logans' land ownership places them outside this dependence, but they are still subject to Granger's scheming when he wants to force them to sell.

Personal possessions also play an important role. Stacey fails to keep the new coat that is a valuable item in itself, and a token of Hammer's love. The glamour of possessing an expensive thing, and showing it off, is represented by TJ's flaunting of the coat once he has tricked Stacey out of it. Even more, it is represented by the pearl-handled pistol that TJ so wants, and by the gifts the Simms boys supposedly give him, which he pathetically regards as tokens of the high esteem in which they hold him.

Boost your learning

?   Make a large table using the theme names, or icons, across the top and down one side. Add notes to its boxes to show how the themes connect. Example: in the box at the intersection of 'Family-community' and 'Property', you could write, 'Logan land'.

?   Test yourself by using the Mini Mind Map and full Mind Map, as suggested at the start of this section.

take a break before attacking the blow-by-blow account

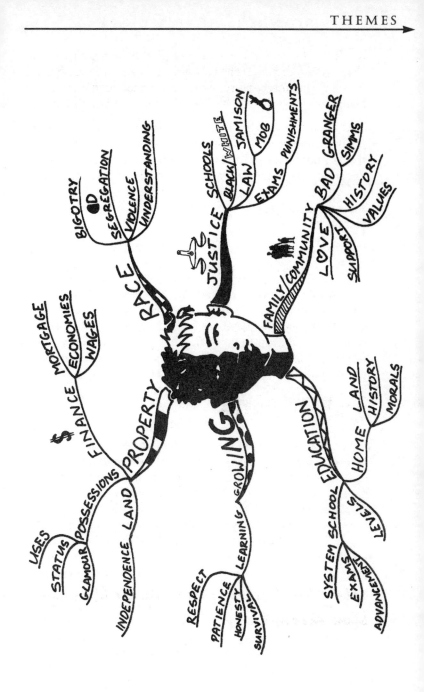

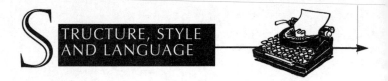
Structure

The **structure** of a novel is the overall pattern of its plot. To see it, you need to 'stand back' from the details. The structure of *Roll of Thunder* works in two ways:

1 as a series of cycles, in each of which tension *mounts, climaxes* and *relaxes* (MCR);
2 as an *interweaving* and *development* of separate *threads* (IDT).

Looking at the first way, we find that although injustice is highlighted in Chapter 1, the real tension starts in Chapter 2, when we suspect that Papa has brought Mr Morrison to protect the family from a growing threat. This threat mounts, climaxing in Chapter 3 when the Ku Klux Klan appear. The tension relaxes a little when we learn that the Klan were not looking for the Logans. Another climax comes in Chapter 5 when Cassie has such a hard time in Strawberry.

After the short-lived peace of Christmas in Chapter 7, tension mounts again, and never really lets up until the final chapter. There is a 'warning' climax in Chapter 9, when the Wallaces attack, then the main climax, spread over the final two chapters, and dying off with the last embers of the fire at the end of Chapter 12.

The separate threads in the structure can be identified as:

- injustice – made obvious in Chapter 1;
- the mounting threat of violence – especially in Chapters 2, 3, 5, 9 and 11;
- lessons learned by the children – Little Man in Chapter 1, Stacey in Chapters 4 and 7, and Cassie in Chapters 5 and 8;
- the battle of the boycott – as Granger and the Wallaces pile on the pressure and things get tougher for the Logans, especially in Chapters 7–10.
- TJ's decline and fall, beginning in Chapter 8 when Mary Logan fails him, he gets her fired, and he is shunned.

You should also be aware that the narrative is continuous – there are no big gaps or time-shifts, and that it covers almost a year, from October to the end of the following summer, with Christmas falling in Chapter 7.

Style

The novel is written in **first-person narrative** – as if Cassie is addressing us directly. This helps us to become quickly involved in the novel, and particularly with Cassie. It also enables Mildred Taylor to give a vivid impression of Cassie's emotions, one example being when Cassie is terrified by the Ku Klux Klan (Ch. 3).

One disadvantage of first-person narrative is that the author cannot comment on the action or characters, or explain background. This has to be done either by nine-year-old Cassie or by characters speaking to her. Hence the scenes in which adults tell her about the Logan land, or about black history. The other disadvantage is that Cassie can tell us only those bits of the story that she experiences, or hears about, so she has to do a lot of spying and eavesdropping on adult conversations to keep us informed. Sometimes we just have to guess – as when Mr Morrison talks Hammer out of challenging Simms.

Another feature of this novel is the use of setting to create atmosphere; for example the forest or the Wallace store. Several passages of skilful description set key scenes (for example, at the start of Chapter 5). Linked to this is the use of the seasons and the weather. The weather plays an active part in Chapters 1 and 3, with the dry red dust turning to mud. It also reflects or warns us of violence. The Wallaces attack the Logan wagon at night, in a storm. Hot, stifling weather leads up to TJ's disastrous break-in, and at the end of Chapter 11, thunder crashes *against the corners of the world* and lightning splits the sky. When the rain comes, it helps put out the fire.

The final style point to note is the use of imagery, especially similes. One example is when Stacey leaps *like a forest fox* (p. 73). Others are noted in the Commentary. Look out for imagery in the novel. Ask yourself how well each **image** works.

Language

The narrative is in standard English, with just the occasional use of a word that may seem strange to English readers. However, much of the story is told through dialogue, and the characters speak their own versions of Southern dialect. This varies from standard English in its grammar, and sometimes its vocabulary. For example, Moe Turner says, *'And TJ know it too. That's why he lit outa here like he done'* (p. 71). Here, *lit* (fled) is a difference in vocabulary, and *done* (did) is a difference in grammar. The word *outa* (out of) is Mildred Taylor's way of showing accent by spelling.

The speech furthest from standard English comes from the older and poorer black characters. Mrs Berry's English is very non-standard. Mary Logan, who is educated, speaks in a more standard style than David, but Mr Granger speaks in a *folksy dialect*, despite his college education. His speech, and that of poorer whites, has much in common with that of the black characters, for example the use of *ain't* and *y'all*.

Focus your learning

? Turn a sheet of paper sideways. Rule it into twelve columns – one for each chapter. In red pen or pencil, draw the novel's 'tension graph'. Add keywords for highs and lows.

? If you were rewriting the novel as third person narrative, able to see and describe whatever you wanted, what extra scenes would you include? Outline three.

time for you to have a change of scene – take a break

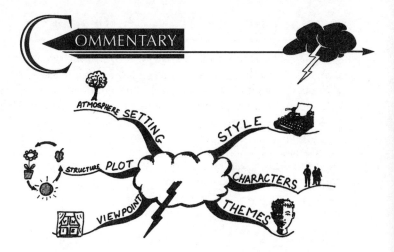

COMMENTARY

The Commentary looks at each chapter in turn, beginning with a brief preview which will prepare you for the chapter and help in revision. The Commentary comments on whatever is important in the chapter, focusing on the areas shown in the Mini Mind Map above.

ICONS

Wherever there is a focus on a particular theme, the icon for that theme appears in the margin (see p. xi for key). Look out, too, for the 'Style and language' sections. Being able to comment on style and language will help you to get an 'A' in your exam.

You will learn more from the Commentary if you use it alongside the novel itself. Read a chapter from the novel, then the corresponding Commentary section – or the other way around.

STARRED QUESTIONS

Remember that when a question appears in the Commentary with a star ✪ in front of it, you should stop and think about it for a moment. And **do remember to take a break** after completing each exercise!

1 Back to school – the dusty road 🖌️

(To p. 18, *our own school*)

◆ The Logan children head for school.
◆ We hear about the Logan land.
◆ TJ explains that the Berrys have been burned.
◆ Little Man gets dirty.
◆ Jeremy Simms is introduced.

The first part of Chapter 1 introduces the main child characters in the novel, and shows some of the relationships between them. It also raises most of the main themes. ❂ Can you remember what they are? Look out for their icons as you read.

The novel begins with Cassie, the narrator, hurrying her little brother. This creates a lively opening and makes us curious about the children, and where they are going. The focus is on Little Man, who is lagging behind. His reason gives us an immediate 'handle' on his character: he is trying *to keep the rusty Mississippi dust* from spoiling his clothes. He is *meticulously neat* – and this will be his first day at school.

We learn something of Cassie's character when she threatens Little Man with the beating he will get if he makes them late. We also discover that on this *bright August-like October morning* she would rather be in the forest in old clothes than going to school in her Sunday-best. Only Little Man is looking forward to school.

We are introduced to Cassie's older brother Stacey. He has become *irritatingly sour* lately, largely because he does not want to be taught by his mother. Understanding this, Cassie restrains herself, but she cannot resist commenting: *'it ain't my fault ...'* This is the first of many times when we see Cassie blurt out her views.

Christopher-John's sensitivity makes him try to copy Stacey's mood in sympathy. Stacey snaps at Cassie and Christopher-John whistles nervously. Cassie grudgingly obeys Stacey – as elsewhere in the novel, then trudges along *in moody silence*. ❂ How would you sum up the likely thoughts and feelings of each child at this point?

The narrative now breaks away to a passage describing the scenery, and then to the history of the land described. Picture the *sun-splotched road* winding *like a lazy red serpent* between the forest on one side and the *giant green and purple stalks* of the cotton field on the other. This passage sets the scene and introduces a vital theme: land ownership and the independence that it brings.

The 'history lesson' explains that the Logan land once belonged to the wealthy white Granger family. After the Civil War, the Grangers had been obliged to sell it to a *Yankee* (a northerner). Grandpa Logan had managed to buy 200 acres in 1887, and then another 200 after the First World War. The Logans are paying off a mortgage (a long-term loan on property) on half their land, and taxes on all of it, so they need a regular income. It also gives the white-owned bank power over them. The paragraph beginning, *I looked at Papa strangely* (p. 12) shows what the land means to the Logans. It also cleverly mentions them all by name, giving details of those we have not yet met. ✪ What do we learn about each person?

Next, TJ Avery appears, followed by his brother Claude. We see TJ's cheerfulness, but also his dishonesty. He is prepared to cheat in school tests and to lie to his parents to get out of trouble at Claude's expense. Even when he tells the story of the burning, he tries to manipulate his audience for maximum attention. ✪ How well does this work?

The burning is a particularly nasty example of racism, but even on the way to school the children experience racist injustice in a milder form. The white students' bus suddenly appears *spewing clouds of red dust like a huge yellow dragon breathing fire* (p. 16). Little Man is covered with dust. The white students laugh. ✪ How does TJ react, and how do Stacey and Cassie react to him?

Jeremy Simms is a very different kind of white boy. He greets Stacey *shyly*. Although he is unconfident, and obeys his sister Lillian Jean, he is prepared to suffer beatings from his father for associating with black children.

The last paragraph describes the school for whites – Jefferson Davis County School. Remember this description when you read about the school for blacks. ✪ What does the relative positioning of the flags suggest about the school's loyalties?

Getting to know the characters

? Who speaks each line below, and what does it tell us about the speaker and his or her relationships with other characters? (Answers on p. 73.)

1 *'Me, I'm gonna stay clean.'*
2 *'Cassie, stop that.'*
3 *'Look out there, Cassie girl. All that belongs to you.'*
4 *'You'll be learnin' all sorts of stuff 'fore the rest of us ... . Like what's on all them tests.'*
5 *'It might hurt y'all's little ears.'*
6 *'Ah, boy, don't start that mess again.'*
7 *'Come on, Claude, let's go on ahead.'*
8 *''Cause they like to see us run and it ain't our bus.'*

? Try 'hot-seating' with a friend. Take it in turns to assume the role of a character while your partner asks questions: e.g. 'TJ, how do you feel about getting Claude a beating?' If working alone, write down the questions and answers, or make a Mind Map.

take a break – then it's back to school

Ragged books cause a rumpus

(From p. 18, *The Great Faith Elementary*, to end of chapter)

◆ Miss Crocker addresses the new class.
◆ Little Man and Cassie refuse their school books.
◆ Mama explains to Miss Crocker.

We have just seen the Jefferson Davis County School, a *long white wooden building* with a *wide sports field* and an *expansive front lawn*. Now we see the Great Faith Elementary and Secondary School, which is *dismal* by comparison. ✪ How many students are there per teacher? ✪ What kind of lawnmower does the school have? The school buildings cluster round a small church – black schools were mostly funded by the black churches. Now the church bell rings to warn the students that school starts in five minutes.

Little Man pushes his way to the well. ✪ Why do you suppose he does this? Cassie sits on the step, her body language telling us how she feels about being back at school. She takes out her mood on the principal's daughter, who is the only girl wearing a new dress. Cassie is not alone in feeling uncomfortable in Sunday clothes. They will be packed away after this first day of school.

Although Cassie would rather not be at school, some students, including Moe Turner (p. 20), walk seven hours each day to get an education. Cassie, as the narrator, expresses her feelings about this amusingly: *I don't think my feet would have wanted that badly for me to be educated.* ✪ Why should education be so important to some students, or at least to their parents?

Little Man, now looks reasonably smart again, which prompts Cassie to make a half-hearted attempt to clean herself up. She goes in at the last possible moment, and takes a seat that two girls had been saving for the principal's daughter.

Miss Daisy Crocker, the first adult we meet, is a pale-skinned, bulging-eyed black woman. She glares at Cassie even before she does anything wrong, speaks *primly*, walks *stiffly* and smiles *mechanically*. The first and fourth graders are in one classroom for now – which is why Cassie and Little Man are together. Notice how Miss Crocker addresses the new students: *'I'll have the pleasure of sprinkling your little minds with the first rays of knowledge.'* ✪ What would you think of her?

Miss Crocker insists on the students promising her as a group to *'work, work, work … and share, share, share.'* ✪ Would you share Cassie's attitude to such group responses? Miss Crocker requires another group promise: *'We promise to take good care of our new books!'*

Cassie is briefly *somewhat excited* at the prospect of the books. Little Man is even more so. But they are a big disappointment. The pictures in them are of *Girls with blond braids and boys with blue eyes*, and the books are in very poor condition. Worst of all, as Little Man discovers, a chart inside (p. 26) makes it clear that the county considers the books unfit for white children, but good enough for blacks. When Little

Man furiously rejects his book, Cassie tries to explain to Miss Crocker. ✪ What does Miss Crocker's cold reply (*'That's what you are'*) reveal about her attitude to racism? What do we learn about Cassie?

The final scene of the chapter takes place in Mama's classroom. Since the story is narrated by Cassie, Mildred Taylor has to make her spy on the two teachers through the doorway. ✪ How successful do you find this narrative device? This is the first we see of Mama, although we have heard a lot about her already. Notice that she does not assume that her fellow teacher is in the right, although she says that Miss Crocker had a right to punish the children. ✪ Why? How far do you agree?

We learn that Mary Logan has taught at the school for fourteen years, but is still regarded by some as a disruptive influence. One piece of dialogue (p. 30) highlights her attitude to racism, compared with Miss Crocker's:

> *'Well, I just think you're spoiling those children, Mary. They've got to learn how things are sometime.'*
> *'Maybe so ... but that doesn't mean they have to accept them ... and maybe we don't either.'*

Education for all

? Fill in the chart below to show how Great Faith differs from your own school.

Buildings	Sports facilities	Class sizes	Books	Racial mix	Punishments

? The wordsearch below contains words that might describe Mary Logan, Daisy Crocker, or both. Use coloured pens to mark the words and who they describe. (Words revealed on p. 73.)

X	B	T	F	U	E	L	C	Q	S	P	B
O	P	O	D	N	B	F	O	T	T	R	R
L	A	L	I	O	R	A	N	B	R	O	O
Z	T	I	O	R	A	B	S	T	I	F	F
P	R	E	T	T	Y	C	E	L	C	E	D
R	O	K	T	H	P	D	R	A	T	S	I
K	N	J	R	O	R	K	V	L	W	S	L
Y	I	R	A	D	I	C	A	L	F	I	L
A	Z	M	I	O	M	N	T	T	O	O	N
D	I	N	N	X	F	A	I	R	A	N	O
R	N	B	E	B	X	N	V	N	K	A	P
F	G	C	D	Y	K	K	E	E	N	L	S

school's over, so take a break and prepare to meet a human tree

2 Papa brings Mr Morrison home

◆ Papa brings Mr Morrison to stay.
◆ He is welcomed into the Logan home.
◆ We hear about John Henry Berry's death.
◆ Papa says that the Logans don't shop at the Wallace store, and tells the children not to go there.

Like Chapter 1, this chapter begins with a short speech arousing our curiosity. It is spoken by Big Ma, a physically powerful woman, with skin the reddish brown of a pecan nut shell. She, Mama and the children are picking cotton (although Mama is a teacher!). Cassie spies two figures approaching.

One is Papa, who runs *swiftly, easily, like the wind* towards the children. The other, a *human tree,* is Mr Morrison. This man, who is over 7 feet tall, with muscles to match, has lost his job because of a fight started by white men. Papa has brought him to work for the family – but also, it is hinted, to protect them.

The Logan front room is *a warm, comfortable room of doors and wood and pictures.* The photographs emphasize the importance of family to the Logans, and reveal that Papa's two older brothers are dead. The furniture, crafted by family members, conveys a sense of respectability and family history.

Mr Morrison speaks in *a deep, quiet voice like the roll of low thunder.* ✪ What does this echo of the title suggest to you about the part that he is to play? After Mama has told him that she is glad to have him there *'especially now'*, the children wonder whether trouble is brewing – and so do we.

It is revealed that John Henry Berry, burned by white men, has died. The children learn the full story by eavesdropping on the adults. John Henry and his brother Beacon have been pursued by two white men who claim to think that one of them was flirting with a white woman. ✪ Do you think this allegation is true? Running low on petrol, the brothers take refuge with

 their aunt and uncle, but the white men set fire to all three men.

We also hear of a recent lynching. The racism is getting worse. The children cannot understand the connection when Papa says, *'In this family, we don't shop at the Wallace store.'* If you've read the rest of the novel, you should know why. Papa tells them to avoid the store, because of the smoking and illegal drinking that goes on there, and because of the sort of people the Wallaces are. ○ What do you think of his method of enforcing his ban? (See the last line.)

Boost your learning

? To whom do the following lines refer? (Answers on p. 73.)
1 *tall and strongly built ... clear, smooth skin ... the colour of a pecan shell*
2 *too heavy now to climb the poles*
3 *tawny-coloured, thin and sinewy, with delicate features in a strong-jawed face*
4 *the easy fluid gate of the shorter man*
5 *the most formidable-looking being we had ever encountered*
6 *square, high-cheekboned face*
7 *his pudgy hands filled with dried corn ... his lower lip quivering*
8 *a frail, sickly man with a hacking cough*

? Make Mini Mind Maps on (a) the range of feelings that the black church-goers might have about the burning, and (b) what options they have, in your view.

3 The bus trap – and night-time terror

◆ Heavy rain turns the dust to mud.
◆ The school bus gives the children another mud-bath.
◆ They set a trap and get their revenge.
◆ News comes that the Ku Klux Klan are *riding.*
◆ Cassie is terrified by approaching cars.

This chapter focuses on two incidents: the Logan children's revenge on the bus driver and his passengers, and the chilling arrival of the Ku Klux Klan – the *devilish night men*. (Remember: Ku, not Klu.) These incidents are not linked – except in the fears of the children, but dramatically the moods of the two episodes contrast strongly. Sandwiched between them is a brief lull of comic relief and relaxation. Remember the sequence as the three Rs – Revenge, Relief, Riders.

THE SCHOOL BUS

The weather features strongly in this chapter. The heavy autumn rain is turning the red dust to mud. Notice how Mildred Taylor personifies the dust at *rejoicing in its own resiliency* – its strength to resist, at first laughing at the rain, then being *forced to surrender*. Remember this image as you read on, and see whether it **foreshadows** what happens.

The children are soaked by the rain each day, preferring not to wear the smelly calfskins Mama gives them. They are also soaked, as often as not, by the school bus. When Mama explains to Little Man that the county provides no buses for black students, the injustice of it affects him deeply. He becomes more embittered with each day. ❂ How would you feel?

The final straw comes soon. Stacey has acted on TJ's advice and led his brothers and sister down from the bank, where they have gone to avoid the bus. It turns out that the engine they heard was only Mr Granger's *sleek silver Packard* – a status symbol that will become important later on.

Minutes later they are *skidding like frightened puppies* to avoid the bus. It hurtles dangerously towards them, forcing them into the gully. Little Man, *chest-deep in water*, is furious. *Moronic laughter* comes from the bus. Stacey, outraged, comforts Little Man and promises him to stop it happening again. There is a sad moment when Jeremy appears, pleased to see the black children, then sympathetic. ❂ Why do they refuse to speak to him? And why do you think Jeremy never rides the school bus?

Stacey takes charge and organizes a bold act of revenge. Sensibly saying nothing to the unreliable TJ, he gets the water-trap in the road dug, and everyone back for afternoon school. Later they lie in wait, out of sight, and watch the returning bus approach the *man-made lake*. There is irony and dramatic tension as the white students squeal with delight, and as the bus hits the trap hard, almost overturns, and ends up *like a lopsided billy goat on its knees*. ✪ How appropriate is this image?

For Cassie and her brothers, revenge is sweet. Even Mama and Big Ma admit to being pleased about the 'accident'. That evening the children can hardly contain their hilarity whenever they think about the bus. Mama distributes them around the room to get on with their homework.

THE NIGHT MEN

The hush that now descends is a classic thriller-style preparation for a dramatic change of mood. Read the paragraph on p. 53, beginning *The room grew quiet again*. We hear only Big Ma's humming, the fire crackling, and the patter of the rain. This peace is broken by rapid knocking on the door: TJ's father brings a nervous warning that the Ku Klux Klan are riding tonight. The children are sent to bed, and have to glean what information they can through the door. Convinced that the Klan are coming after them because of the school bus incident, they start to panic. Even Stacey is tense, blaming himself.

STYLE AND LANGUAGE

From *Then Big Ma stood up*, through to the end of the chapter, the tension mounts. Mildred Taylor handles the suspense expertly, with a sequence of alarms, false alarms, false comfort, and then the icy reality of the ghostly procession of cars moving down the road towards the Logan house.

Notice how the atmosphere is built up. An 'alarm bell' is sounded by the one-line paragraph after Cassie goes to Big Ma's chair: *She wasn't there*. ✪ Why is this effective? It is *nightly dark*; an owl hoots; water drips; Cassie is *transfixed* (paralysed) with fear. She hears a sound and cannot stop trembling – then feels relief, thinking it must come from the boys; then she is paralysed again when *a scratchy bristlyness* springs on her. Then relief returns – it was the family dog. Just as we start to relax, headlights appear, *like cat eyes*. A man slowly walks up the drive. Cassie stops breathing; so do we. But the moment passes – the cars retreat.

The sense of the now-ebbing danger is accentuated by the image of Mr Morrison *moving silently, like a jungle cat ... a shotgun in his hand.* ○ Have you ever felt anything like Cassie's *waves of sick terror*? Why do you think they come *after* the main moment of danger seems to have passed?

In this passage the first-person narrative works at its best, allowing us into Cassie's fearful anticipation at first hand.

Focus on Cassie

? The words below describe Cassie's changing mood in this chapter. Work out when you could use each word. You can use a word more than once. Either write the words where appropriate in the margin of your copy of the novel, or write them out with notes to explain what point in the chapter they refer to.

angry   frustrated   puzzled   bored
surprised   hopeful   delighted   happy
light-hearted   engrossed   disgruntled
frightened   relieved   terrified

? Imagine you're making a film of the last part of the chapter, as described under 'Style and language' above. Use sketches or brief notes to make a storyboard showing the key shots you would use to bring out the suspense and convey Cassie's experience.

Cassie's had a learning experience, but to improve yours, take a break before reading about Stacey's

4 Stacey takes the rap for TJ – and grows up a little

(To p. 75, *the distance between them fading*)

◆ Mama and Big Ma wonder what's wrong with Cassie.
◆ TJ reveals that Sam Tatum has been tarred and feathered.
◆ Stacey resents Mr Morrison.
◆ Stacey gets whipped by Mama for having TJ's cheat notes.
◆ Stacey fights TJ at the Wallace store and is stopped by Mr Morrison.

The first half of this chapter focuses on the Logan children's anxiety about the Ku Klux Klan, and on Stacey learning to respect Mr Morrison. It begins with Cassie churning butter. Mama and Big Ma are concerned because she seems feverish and wants to stay in and help them rather than play outside. ✪ Why is she like this?

Mama sends Cassie in with the boys. This enables her to hear some news from TJ – so we hear the news as well. TJ plays his usual trick of holding back information in an attempt to make his audience hang on his every word. The Logan children, however, feign *disinterest* (in Britain one would say 'a lack of interest').

TJ recounts his story of the Klan tarring and feathering Sam Tatum for calling a white store-owner a liar. This store-owner, Jim Lee Barnett, becomes important in the plot later on. Note, too, the grim humour in Little Man's concern that if he and the other children were tarred and feathered they would *never get clean again*. ✪ What would it be like? Remember, tar has to be hot to melt.

We see the dishonest side to TJ's character again when he makes an excuse to sneak back and look for Mrs Logan's test questions – which feature later on.

We hear that Mr Morrison now lives in a rundown, rat-infested shack near the Logan house, because he likes his privacy. Stacey resents Mr Morrison and regards his presence as unnecessary. ✪ Why does Stacey feel this? The other children like Mr Morrison.

39

Stacey wants to protect his family. He even tries to protect TJ from his own foolish dishonesty, by tearing up TJ's *cheat notes* (which in Britain might be called a 'crib sheet'). Stacey has a lot to learn – though not in quite the sense that TJ has! We soon discover that Stacey has been whipped for having TJ's new set of cheat notes on his desk. Read Little Willie's account (p. 70) to remind yourself how they got there. Imagine how humiliating it would feel, at Stacey's age, to be whipped (caned) by your own mother in front of the whole class.

Stacey's desire for revenge once again has dangerous consequences. He defies his parents' ruling by going to find TJ at the Wallace store. The other Logan children follow him – to *see what he gonna do* (p. 71). ✪ In terms of Mildred Taylor's narrative, why is it necessary for Cassie to follow Stacey?

The Wallace store, *a small building with a gas pump in front and a storage house in back*, does not sound very exciting. Nor does its clientele seem to have much wit or charm. The white men sitting around stare at the Logan children. Melvin Simms comments, *'Just look at all the little niggers come to dance.'*

Stacey quickly finds TJ and leaps on him *like a forest fox*. They fight, TJ tricking Stacey into letting down his guard. The children are *engrossed* by the spectacle of the fight, until the shouting stops:

Mr Morrison towered above us.

Note the dramatic effect of the one-line paragraph. (Try it yourself sometime!)

Mr Morrison ignores the white men as he takes the children to the wagon. On the way home he considers whether to tell Mrs Logan about the incident. When he says that he won't, Stacey suspects a catch, and he's right: Mr Morrison is going to leave it to Stacey to tell her. Note that Mr Morrison accepts that *'Sometimes a person's gotta fight,'* but adds that a white man's store is not the place for it. ✪ How far do you agree?

Stacey, for some reason that Cassie cannot understand, decides to tell Mama. ✪ Why does he? He and Mr Morrison smile at each other in understanding. ✪ What has changed between them?

Focus your learning

? Make a Mini Mind Map of what Stacey has learned so far in this chapter.

? TJ says, *'Man, that sho' ain't right! I wouldn't do you that way!'* This is an example of the 'non-standard English' that the children usually speak. Find at least another four examples. Divide a page into three columns. Write the examples in column 1, and a standard English version in column 2. In the final column, write out the version you would use if speaking to a friend.

? Write or role-play how Melvin Simms might describe the fight.

now you've seen Stacey grow up a little, take a break before reading about Mama's response

Why the Logans don't shop at the Wallace store

(From *As we neared the house* to end of chapter)

◆ Big Ma tells Cassie more about the Logan land.
◆ Stacey confesses.
◆ Mama takes the children to see the Berrys.
◆ She encourages other families to avoid the Wallace store.

Mr Granger's car pulls away from the Logan house. He has been trying to get Big Ma to sell him Logan land. ○ Why does he want it? (Think back to Chapter 1.) Big Ma and Cassie go into the Logan forest and sit by Caroline pond, named after Big Ma, next to a clearing made when a white man had pressurized Big Ma to sell the lumber. She tells Cassie more about the history of the Logan land. Her late husband Paul Edward bought the first 200 acres from a Yankee called Hollenbeck, and the second from Wade Jamison in 1918. As you read this passage (pp. 77–80), look out for indications that Cassie has heard the story before. ❂ What does this tell us about Big Ma's attitude to the land? Why would Mildred Taylor want us to know its history?

Stacey confesses to going to the Wallace store. Mama guesses that the others have been there too. They are surprised not to get a whipping. However, the next day she awakes them before dawn to go and visit a sick man, telling them not to be afraid of his appearance. After almost two hours they reach the *small weather-grayed house* and barren fields of the Berrys.

Mrs Berry is *an elderly woman, frail and toothless.* Her arm appears to have been broken long ago, never having mended. ❂ Why do you think she didn't have it set in hospital? Despite her misfortunes, Mrs Berry is cheerful and welcoming.

STYLE AND LANGUAGE

Mrs Berry speaks in a similar style to the Logans, but with even more accent and dialect. *Land sakes* is a corruption of 'For the Lord's sake', used in the same way as her *Lord a'mighty.* She speaks about herself modestly as *these old bones.* The grammar of her dialect changes past tenses; for example, *'I jus' sez ...'* ('I just said ...') and *'who ... done come to see 'bout us?'* (who ... has come to see about us?). Some words are omitted; for example, *'Who you reckon comin' to see ...'* misses out 'do' and 'is'. Verb participles also change, as in *'Sho' is!'* ('They surely are!'). ❂ Why is her English further from standard English than that of the Logans?

The sight that greets the Logans is horrific and pitiful. The old man's hair and face are burned away. He cannot speak. Mama talks to both the Berrys about local news for an hour, as if Mr Berry were quite normal. ❂ What do you think of her ability to do this? How good a lesson will this be to the children?

On the way home, the Logans stop at other black homes, so that Mama can ask parents not to let their children visit the Wallace store. Even more important to the

plot, she begins talking about *finding another store to patronize*.
✪ Why does she not directly accuse the Wallaces of murder?

It is important that you understand Mr Turner's predicament (pp. 84–6). He is a 'sharecropper', growing cotton on Mr Montier's land. In place of rent, Montier takes half the crop for himself. Turner is allowed to take goods on credit at the store, with Montier 'signing' for him – guaranteeing payment to the store. Montier sells the other half of the crop and pays off the store, charging Turner a percentage for acting as guarantor. Turner never gets any cash. He is lucky to break even – not owing money to Montier – at the end of the year.

This system suits the white landowner and store-owner very well. That is why it is dangerous for the Logans to challenge it.
✪ What are their motives? Would you consider taking the same risk in their place?

Drive it all home

? Complete the chart below to show the history of the Logan land.

1865–75	Hollenbeck buys from the _____ family.
1887	Paul Edward buys 200 _____ from _____.
1910	Paul Edward pays off the _____.
1918	Paul Edward buys another _____ acres from Mr Wade _____.
1933	Mr _____ lumbermen fell some of the forest.

? Make a Mini Mind Map of what you have learned about Mama in this chapter.

now you know why Stacey escaped a whipping, take some time off before we visit Strawberry

5 Strife in Strawberry

- ◆ Big Ma takes Cassie, Stacey and TJ to the market at Strawberry.
- ◆ Cassie is discriminated against in the Barnett Mercantile.
- ◆ Cassie bumps into Lillian Jean, is pushed, and has to apologize.

This is a chapter of harsh lessons for Cassie. At the start of the chapter she is pleased that Big Ma is finally taking her and Stacey to the market 22 miles away in Strawberry, then disappointed to learn that TJ is coming.

STYLE AND LANGUAGE

A skilful piece of description tells us that TJ is his usual self, despite a sleepy start: *... by dawn, when the December sun was creeping warily upward shooting pale streams of buff-colored light through the forest, he was fully awake and chattering like a cockatoo.* Here Mildred Taylor uses **personification** (see Glossary). In the description of Strawberry in the next paragraph the plain style matches the dullness of the place. The words *sad, spindly, splotched, gloomy* and *sagging* all convey an impression of a depressing little town. The one image is the **metaphor** of the road fleeing out of it, as if anxious to escape.

Cassie's first lesson comes from the inferior position in which Big Ma is obliged to park the wagon, on the far side of the field. This reflects the inferior position of black people in the community. Cassie is angry and cannot accept this. After a lunch of sausages, maize flour bread (maize is also called 'corn on the cob') and curdled milk, the Logans pack up and head into town. Big Ma goes to see the lawyer Mr Jamison, whom Cassie admits to liking because he treats her family with respect and gives straight answers. ❂ Who is the one other likeable white person in the novel? (See 'Who's who?')

Trouble starts to brew when TJ suggests they save time by going into the mercantile (general store) and doing Big Ma's shopping. Stacey thinks about it *for a long moment,* then agrees. ❂ When else has Stacey been persuaded by TJ? What happened then? (Think about mud and buses!) We soon see the store's real attraction for TJ: a pearl-handled revolver, displayed on red velvet. There is tragic irony when he says, *'I'd sell my life for that gun. One of these days I'm gonna have it, too.'* ✪ What reason does he give for wanting it? If you've read the whole novel you will know that this is particularly ironic.

The store-owner, Mr Barnett, hardly treats black people as human, let alone as equals. He breaks off from filling TJ's order to serve a white woman. When he breaks off a second time and is still serving a white girl several minutes later, Cassie thinks he must have forgotten TJ. When Barnett ignores her polite enquiry, she tugs his sleeve. Imagine his outrage – she has dared to touch him!

Barnett's *low, tight voice* explodes into a bellow. Cassie screams back, *'I ain't nobody's little nigger! And you ought not be waiting on everybody 'fore you wait on us.'* The situation is perilous. ✪ Do you admire Cassie, or just feel she is slow to catch on? Barnett tells Stacey *with hateful force* to keep Cassie out of the shop till she knows *what she is*. Cassie retorts, *'I already know what I am!'* This line is a key to her character, and to the novel. ✪ What *is* she – that Barnett fails to see?

Cassie is prevented from seriously insulting the shopkeeper only by Stacey's quick action. Outside the shop, he comments on Barnett's being wrong: *'I know it and you know it, but he don't know it, and that's where the trouble is.'* This identifies the root problem as ignorance: most of the whites fail to understand that black people are human beings, equal to themselves except in the opportunities that society gives them.

Emotionally bruised and humiliated from this encounter, poor Cassie then has the misfortune to bump into Lillian Jean Simms on the sidewalk (raised wooden pavement). Cassie apologizes, but this is not enough for the white girl, despite Jeremy's well-meaning but feeble attempt to intervene. When Lillian Jean tries to push Cassie off the sidewalk, Cassie pulls back her arm – to find it grabbed and twisted by Mr Simms, who pushes her off, so that she lands *bottom first on the ground.* ✪ How would passers-by react if this occurred in your local shopping mall?

Cassie receives no sympathy from the people who start to gather. Jeremy tries again to intervene, but to no avail. Then Big Ma appears and makes Cassie apologize. ✪ Is Big Ma right to do this?

What have you learned?

?   Who might say each of these lines to a news reporter? (Answers on p. 73.)

1 *'I almost wanted to disown her, but I knew I couldn't.'*
2 *'We jus' tryin' to help out, get that ol' order filled.'*
3 *'Niggers are lucky we let 'em in at all.'*
4 *'It's hard on the child, but she has to learn.'*
5 *'No nigger gal gonna stand in my gal's way.'*
6 *'I tried, b-but Pa gets real mean ...'*

?   Use the words below on the main branches of a Mind Map. Add to it to show at what points in the chapter the words might describe Cassie's feelings.

disappointed   angry   afraid   excited   humiliated
bored   outraged   incredulous

?   Write an entry for Lillian Jean's diary for the market day in Strawberry.

6 Will Simms get Hammered?

◆ Uncle Hammer is home.
◆ Cassie tells him about Mr Simms.
◆ Hammer intends to teach Simms a lesson – but Mr Morrison goes with him.
◆ Cassie remonstrates with Ma and receives a history lesson.
◆ Hammer and Mr Morrison return, bleary-eyed.
◆ As the family dress for church, Hammer gives Stacey a new coat.
◆ At church, TJ teases Stacey about the coat.
◆ The Wallaces mistake Hammer's car for Granger's.

Cassie, Stacey, TJ and Big Ma travel home in silence. As Cassie and Stacey put away the mule, Stacey offers Cassie some kind advice. He explains that Big Ma had to make Cassie apologize. His efforts are cut short when they discover a car in the barn. At first they think it's Mr Granger's, but when they go indoors they find it belongs to *a tall, handsome man, nattily dressed in a gray pin-striped suit and vest.* It's their Uncle Hammer!

The children are excited to see Hammer. He is a warm, generous man, although his eyes often have *a cold, distant glaze* and he has *an aloofness in him* which keeps the children slightly at a distance. ❂ Is this part of his basic character, or the result of his experiences? (Consider this as you read on.) He also has a wicked sense of humour, revealed as he explains why he bought a car like Mr Granger's – only newer: *'It seems that me and Harlan Granger just got the same taste.'*

Big Ma does her best to keep Cassie from telling Hammer about her day in Strawberry, but hot-headed Cassie continues. Hammer is amused that she has given Mr Barnett a piece of her mind, but coldly furious when he hears about Cassie being knocked off the sidewalk. His eyes ice over in their *cold distant way*. Mama and Big Ma try to hold him back, but he is determined to have it out with Simms. The women send Stacey to fetch Mr Morrison – who manages to jump into the Packard just before Hammer drives off into the night.

The men gone, Cassie remonstrates with her mother about Big Ma making her apologize in Strawberry. Mama explains that Big Ma was trying to protect her. This develops into a full-blown lesson in the history of racial prejudice. White people think they're better than black people. Simms is *'... one of those people who has to believe that white people are better than black people to make himself feel big.'*

Mama explains that in the past, the slave-owners and dealers tried to justify themselves by preaching that black people were not human. They also taught that slavery made blacks into good Christians. When slaves were freed after the Civil War, the prejudice continued. ❂ Why are poor whites like Simms often more violently prejudiced than wealthier whites? (See p. 107.) Can you see any evidence of this in your own community?

Cassie now starts to worry more about her uncle than about Simms getting what he deserves (top of p. 108). Mama's relief when Hammer and Mr Morrison come home allows her to joke about going to church by mule-cart instead of in the Packard. This mood of relief continues as Cassie and Mama prepare for church. Mama is a pretty woman who makes the most of her appearance and does the same for Cassie. We see Cassie's fondness for her mother. Despite Cassie's lesson, she is still disappointed when she learns from Stacey that Hammer has not *whipped Mr Simms.* ✪ Is this what you, as a reader, want to happen?

Now it is Stacey's turn to learn another lesson. It begins when Hammer gives him his Christmas present early. It is a good-quality woollen coat – too big, but still the best coat Stacey has ever had. Stacey is delighted. At church TJ notices Stacey's new coat, and tells Stacey that it makes him look *like a fat preacher.* Part of Stacey knows that TJ is just jealous, but the taunts still affect him, spoiling his pleasure in the coat.

After church, Hammer takes the family for a drive. ✪ Why does Mama persuade him not to drive through Strawberry? Heading back, they approach Soldiers Bridge, named after a Civil War incident. Passing the Wallace store, Hammer talks about burning the place down to avenge the death of his friend John Henry. ✪ Should he?

They approach Soldiers Bridge, where the Logans usually have to back off to allow white people to cross before them. (Imagine getting a mule and wagon to reverse.) Hammer speeds on to the bridge, so that the driver of an old Model-T truck reverses for them. It turns out to contain the Wallaces, who touch their hats respectfully – and then freeze as they realize that the sleek Packard is Hammer's and not Mr Granger's! Hammer is pleased with himself, but Mama says that one day they'll have to pay for angering the Wallaces. ✪ What sort of payment do you expect?

Hammer it home

❓ In what ways do any of the Logan children seem to take after their uncle? Re-read the Commentary for this chapter for clues.

❓ Mind Map the likely arguments used by Mr Morrison to persuade Hammer.

? Mark the following statements 1–5, with 5 for 'Strongly agree' and 0 for 'Strongly disagree', and find at least one piece of evidence to justify each score.

Hammer is a cautious man who thinks carefully before acting. ☐

Mama thinks black people are better than white people. ☐

Stacey appreciates his new coat. ☐

Cassie finds it hard to accept the way blacks are treated. ☐

Hammer likes showing off. ☐

do something different for a while before seeing why hot words leave Stacey cold

7 Merry Christmas – and three white visitors

(To p. 126, 'Then go to sleep. Christmas is coming.')

◆ Stacey has given his coat to TJ – who gets to keep it.
◆ Papa comes home for Christmas.
◆ Mr Morrison tells his story.
◆ The Logan adults discuss backing the families shopping in Vicksburg.

Mama's opening line tells us immediately what the first part of the chapter will be about: Stacey's new coat. Mama says she will take up the sleeves. At first Stacey stalls, but he cannot cover up his guilt for long: he has given the coat to TJ to wear. Mama is furious because the coat was a present from Hammer. She tells Stacey to fetch it back from TJ.

Hammer intervenes sternly, saying that TJ can keep it: *At least he knows a good thing when he sees it.*

This is an important sub-theme of the chapter – knowing the value of a good thing, and hanging on to it.

STYLE AND LANGUAGE

Hammer 'hammers' into Stacey – verbally, in a torrent of rhetorical questions (not expecting an answer), finally asking if Stacey would run *buck naked* down the road if TJ told him to. His next speech, too, is full of angry energy. Try reading both speeches aloud in the voice you think he would use for this *tongue-lashing*.

Hammer drives his lesson home: *'if you want something and it's a good thing and you got it in the right way, you better hang on to it and don't let nobody talk you out of it.'* Bear this in mind as the chapter unfolds.

Cassie is impatient for Christmas. She wants school to finish and she is tired of Lillian Jean flouncing past, and of TJ crowing about his new coat. The weather is bad and she longs for Papa to come home. On the morning of Christmas Eve, she gets her wish. Soon the house is full of the rich aromas of food cooking for Christmas – including, instead of a turkey,

 a gigantic coon (a racoon). ❂ How do the family's Christmas preparations compare with yours?

The atmosphere is relaxed, warm and friendly. But *as the night deepened and the peanuts in the pan grew shallow* (note the contrast), happy memories give way to the bitter tale. Mr Morrison tells of a bleak Christmas shortly after the end of slavery, when he was a child of around six years old, in 1876. Two teenage boys came to the house for help, accused of molesting a white woman. Moments later, *them devilish night men* – the Ku Klux Klan – swept down on the family, *hacking and killing, burning us out*. The parents put up a good fight, flinging six-year-old Mr Morrison to safety before being overpowered. Mr Morrison ends with the line, *I makes myself remember* (p. 123). ❂ Why do you think he does?

Cassie awakes from a disturbed sleep to find that Big Ma, with whom she shares a bed, is not there. It is a little hard to believe that when Cassie creeps into her parents' room she is able to go unnoticed for long enough to hear most of the adult argument about the Wallaces. However, it does mean that as narrator she is able to tell us about it. Mama wants to use their land to back the credit of families boycotting the Wallace store.

Big Ma is anxious. Hammer says, *'I'd rather burn them out myself,'* reinforcing his attitude with an impressively dismissive triple negative: *'Ain't gonna have nothing noway.'* Papa, for his part, shares his wife's feelings but is afraid that if they back the credit they will lose the land. When Cassie seeks reassurance, he tells her: *'We ain't never gonna lose this land.'*

Test your recall (answers on p. 73)

? Mark the correct answer.
Stacey gives the coat to TJ because:
(a) he feels sorry for TJ; (b) he feels silly wearing it;
(c) he loses it in a bet.
Papa has been away:
(a) working on the railroad; (b) visiting the Berrys;
(c) in prison.
Mr Morrison's parents were born:
(a) in Africa; (b) free; (c) on a slave-breeding farm.
? How many people ate Christmas dinner in the Logan home?

mmm ... roasted racoon – take a snack-break!

Three white visitors

(From p. 126, *'Books!' cried Little Man*, to end of chapter)

◆ Christmas Day – presents and a visit from Jeremy.
◆ Mr Jamison offers to back the credit.
◆ Mr Granger puts pressure on the Logans.

Christmas morning comes, and the mood of well-being is restored. The children are delighted to get books – and not ragged ones either. You have probably heard of *The Three Musketeers.* ✪ Did you know that its author was black? Little Man seems particularly happy. He keeps washing his hands in case he gets his book dirty, and is delighted with his new trousers (*pants*) and sweater. Remember the line Mildred Taylor uses: *Little Man, who treasured clothes above all else.* ✪ Which adult does he remind us of in this respect?

Christmas is crowded but joyful. All eight Avery children and their parents come for dinner – a *feast.* Everyone is sitting around the fire when a timid knock on the door is heard. It is a *frozen and very frightened* Jeremy Simms. Hammer is at first outraged, but Papa is more diplomatic. Perhaps, too, having children of his own, he is more sympathetic toward Jeremy. Perhaps, too, he appreciates the courage it must have taken to come.

Cassie as usual puts her foot in it: *'Nuts! Why we got more nuts now than we know what –'* she is cut off by her mother, who gives a kinder and more polite response. In a poignant act of awkward generosity, Jeremy hands Stacey a present – a flute which he has carved himself. ✪ What do you feel about this moment? Are you surprised, relieved, or both, when Stacey thanks Jeremy, and when Papa finds the right way to send Jeremy home without offending him?

Stacey has learnt from his mistake over the new coat. When TJ tries to put him off the flute, Stacey tells him to *stuff it.* TJ takes it as a cue to enthuse about the *little pearl-handled pistol* that he wants so much.

Stacey's conversation with his father about friendship between blacks and whites is an important one for the message of the novel, and for its plot. ✪ Do you agree that friendship has to be based on equality? Papa says, *'Maybe one day whites and blacks can be real friends'* – but not yet. ✪ How easy is it in your community? Stacey puts the flute in *his box of treasured things,* where it will remain untouched, a symbol of hope for a harmony not yet possible.

The next white visitor to call on the Logans is Mr Jamison. He is transferring ownership of the land from Big Ma to her two sons, Hammer and David, so that she cannot be intimidated into selling it. When it seems that Mr Jamison should be leaving, he remains, and raises the subject of the Logans backing the credit of families wanting to shop in Vicksburg.

We have already learned that Mr Jamison is a straight-talking, honest man who treats black people as equals. At the same time, he is realistic and warns the Logans that they may lose their land. Then he offers to back the credit himself. Hammer answers with a *wry sneer*. Undaunted, Mr Jamison spells out his offer in a businesslike way probably calculated to avoid embarrassment. ✪ How would you react if you were one of the Logans?

In a long speech (pp. 134–5), Mr Jamison explains why Harlan Granger resents the Logans. Harlan wants his family land back, he objects to black people being independent, and he cannot accept that whites and blacks should be equal in the eyes of the law: *'Now that is what Harlan Granger absolutely will not permit.'*

The final visitor is Granger himself. He is not openly rude or aggressive, but he acts as if he has every right to be sitting in the Logans' home, smoking his cigar and lecturing them. He speaks to Hammer in a way that is mildly insulting, but with just enough superficial good humour to avoid a confrontation. Hammer gives as good as he gets, scorning the *'fifty cents a day'* that is the top rate for Granger's workers. To give you an idea of what this is worth, the pistol TJ longs for is priced at nearly $35.95. An experienced worker would take 72 days to earn enough to buy the pistol.

Granger seems to be less fiercely bigoted than some of the local whites. As a landowner able to exploit black tenants and cream off a percentage of the Wallace store's profits, he is fairly contented with the way things are. He says to the Logans:

'This is a fine community. Got fine folks in it – both white and coloured. Whatever's bothering you people, y'all just tell me. We'll get it straightened out without all this big to-do.'

✪ How do you view this speech? Does Granger really think that some black people are *fine*? What response does he hope to get? Failing to get a satisfactory answer, he resorts to veiled threats. He may just *have* to charge his tenants more of their crop, and the bank manager Joe Higgins (they are on first-name terms, naturally), won't be able to honour a loan to troublemakers like the Logans. Papa stands firm. Granger hints, *'There's lots of ways of stopping you, David.'* Notice that the words *slyly* and *smugly* are used – very appropriately – to describe his manner.

Boost your learning

❓ Tick the boxes below to show which words describe each character (a word can describe more than one character):

	Jeremy	Mr Jamison	Mr Granger
timid	☐	☐	☐
complacent	☐	☐	☐
brave	☐	☐	☐
generous	☐	☐	☐
fair-minded	☐	☐	☐
greedy	☐	☐	☐
honest	☐	☐	☐
devious	☐	☐	☐
upright	☐	☐	☐
straightforward	☐	☐	☐

❓ What will Jeremy be like as an adult? Write keywords for your views.

8 Revenge

◆ Cassie plots revenge on Lillian Jean.
◆ TJ worries about exams.
◆ Papa advises Cassie about self-respect.
◆ TJ is failed for cheating.
◆ Cassie gets her revenge.
◆ The school board visits – Mama is fired.
◆ Stacey discovers that TJ got her fired.
◆ TJ is shunned.

CASSIE LOGAN GETS EVEN

We have seen Cassie's impulsiveness and fiery temper. Now we see another side to her, as she carefully plots and prepares her revenge on Lillian Jean. Three adverbs show the stages of Lillian Jean's response when Cassie first approaches her, apparently penitent: she reacts *irritably*, *suspiciously* and then *enthusiastically*. Lillian Jean is soon won round by Cassie's simple but loaded statement: *'I'm who I am and you're who you are.'* ❂ What does Lillian Jean take it to mean? What else could it mean?

Little Man and Christopher-John are disgusted by Cassie's ingratiating behaviour (you probably have your own non-standard English phrase for it!). Even Jeremy tells her, *'C-Cassie, you didn't have to do that. That-that ole Lillian Jean, she ain't worth it.'* TJ refers to her *Uncle Tomming* Lillian Jean. (The phrase comes from a character, Uncle Tom, in an anti-slavery novel by white American author Harriet Beecher Stowe.) Only Stacey suspects Cassie's true motives – and so ensures that no one else tells the adults.

TJ is more worried about his school exams than he is about Cassie. Once again, he attempts to get inside information on the questions from Stacey – and is quickly rebuffed. Cassie is *unable to resist just one bit of friendly advice*. Fortunately, the fact that you're reading this guide shows that you've already taken the advice to heart. She tells him, *'Try studying.'*

STYLE AND LANGUAGE

Papa takes Cassie *to the misty hollow where the trees lay fallen.* Here it seems natural that they talk *in quiet, respectful tones, observing the soft mourning of the forest* (p. 142). The last time Cassie sat here with an adult was when Big Ma told her about the Logan land. Notice how setting creates atmosphere and prepares us for what happens. The fact that Papa and Cassie are here, coupled with the tone of the opening paragraph, tells us to expect some quiet reflection and a lesson to be learned. ☻ What do we expect in other settings – for example the Wallace store?

Papa tells Cassie that sometimes in life she will have to go against her own impulses – just to survive. As an example, he explains why he could not give Charlie Simms *a good thrashing* for hurting Cassie. But, he adds, *'There are things you can't back down on, things you gotta take a stand on.'* It is about self-respect, and being able to live with yourself. ☻ Has this ever been an issue for you?

Cassie assures Papa that Charlie Simms will not get involved in whatever she decides to do about Lillian Jean. Then she proceeds to hatch her plan. For a whole month she pretends to be Lillian Jean's devoted servant, carrying her books – and listening respectfully to her secrets. Lillian Jean is entirely taken in.

Meanwhile another strand of the plot is emerging. TJ has been failed in his final exam for cheating. We could simply conclude that he has only himself to blame. But think of what is revealed in the miserably frustrated speech in which he says, *'All y'all Logans think y'all so doggone much with y'all's new coats and books and shiny new Packards!'* ☻ Do you feel any sympathy for him?

Cassie now seizes her opportunity to lead the gullible Lillian Jean to her fate. They are on their way home. The other children have gone on ahead. Lillian Jean appears and the two girls stroll casually (*saunter*) down the road; Lillian Jean has no reason to suspect. But Cassie is *sweeping the road* (with her eyes), looking for the path along which she plans to lead Lillian Jean into the forest. Telling the white girl of a nice surprise in store for her, Cassie leads her to a secluded spot, throws down her books and then beats her up.

Notice that Cassie says, *'For the record, she had hit me first.'*
✪ Do you think Cassie would still have attacked Lillian Jean if she had been unable to provoke her into striking the first blow? Cassie is surprisingly calculating, hitting Lillian Jean only where the bruises will not show. Although at first Lillian Jean tries to be *cute* (clever) and 'sasses' Cassie (answers her back), Cassie gets the better of her and makes her apologize – not just for what she did in Strawberry, but for the whole of Mississippi!

Cassie ensures that Lillian Jean will not tell her father about the incident, by threatening to tell Lillian Jean's friends about her spilling their secrets, and by reminding her what a joke it will be that she got beaten up by a nine-year-old. Cassie's pleasure is spoiled when she realizes that Lillian Jean fails to understand that she has been tricked, and why. Revenge
 is sweet, but not as sweet as Cassie had hoped.
✪ How much of a lesson has she taught Lillian Jean?

MARY LOGAN GETS FIRED

Mildred Taylor makes the next scene-change with a characteristically dramatic line of dialogue. Cassie is in school and Miss Crocker has spotted her daydreaming. Cassie makes a good point – that Miss Crocker repeats herself so much that her pupils need pay attention only for the first few minutes of her lesson. ✪ Do you find this with some teachers?

Conveniently for the story, Cassie is sent to sit at the back, next to the window. This means that she is able to spot Kaleb Wallace – the store owner – walking past. Pretending to need the toilet, Cassie goes out and sees Wallace talking to the school's head teacher and two white men. We must assume that she guesses what is going on, because she then goes and peers into her mother's classroom.

You have probably heard teachers talking about school inspections. What Cassie now sees is an inspection of Mary Logan's teaching – but carried out by three hostile, unqualified, racist men, and without warning. ✪ Ask your teachers how they would feel. Matters are made worse by the fact that she is teaching a lesson about slavery. Mr Granger says that he and the school board members (governors) have come to *learn something*. He is speaking ironically – he doesn't really expect to learn anything. However, this is doubly ironic, because if he was prepared to listen without prejudice then he would indeed learn something.

In front of the class, Mr Granger comments on the pasted over charts on the inside covers, and tells Mary Logan that she shouldn't be teaching things that aren't in the book. She defends herself by saying that *'… all that's in that book isn't true.'* This makes it easy for Granger to make sure that she loses her job.

Mary Logan – Mama – is certainly upset about being fired, but she is not beaten by it. Nor are the other members of her family, who are supportive. Papa is especially reassuring. Mr Morrison offers to look for work and makes it clear in a few words how much he values the Logans as his new-found family.

In the next change of scene we are back at school, where Stacey discovers from Little Willie Wiggins that it was TJ who got Mama fired, by complaining to Kaleb Wallace about her. Stacey wastes no time in finding TJ and confronting him. TJ of course tries to slide out of the accusation, but Stacey by now knows him well enough not to be taken in.

Stacey has matured. Instead of physically attacking TJ he gets all the children to shun him. In British terms he is 'sent to Coventry'. ✪ What effect would this have on a boy like TJ? At first TJ thinks he'll be able to talk the Logans round as in the past. Then, pathetically – but also with a hint of things to come, he reveals that now he has other friends who give him things and treat him like a man. Best of all – they're white! ✪ How do you feel about TJ at this point?

Boost your learning

?   In this chapter both Cassie and TJ are in their different ways motivated by revenge. Make a Mind Map, or write a paragraph, to show what Mildred Taylor's views on revenge seem to be.

?   TJ is a more complex character than he at first seems. Imagine you are his tutor. Make notes for a report suggesting what his problems are and how he could be encouraged to do better at school.

you'll do better if you take a break – before seeing more of a rather timid character

9 Tension mounts – the Wallaces attack

◆ Jeremy sheds light on his family.
◆ TJ is getting into bad company.
◆ Mr Jamison brings a warning.
◆ Mr Avery and Mr Lanier stop shopping at Vicksburg.

◆ Papa, Mr Morrison and Stacey go to Vicksburg.

◆ They are attacked by the Wallaces.

In this short chapter we see tensions mount as the Wallaces try to stop black families taking their custom to the store at Vicksburg. The chapter moves to a climax which is shocking, but which none the less is just a taste of things to come.

STYLE AND LANGUAGE

The chapter begins with a gentle and affectionate description of spring. If you have ever read any novels by Thomas Hardy, the opening paragraph may remind you of the way he sometimes starts a chapter. The image of the chicks seems hopeful, and the final sentence of the paragraph is positively bursting: *Rain-drenched, fresh, vital, full of life, spring enveloped all of us.*

We move on to an exchange between Jeremy and the Logan children. He is thinking about how he will miss them after school finishes for them and he stops seeing them on the road. They are surprised to hear that he will be lonely. They cannot understand at first how he can be lonely with so many brothers and sisters. ✪ What does this tell us about the Logan family life?

This leads Jeremy into telling them about his older brothers laughing at TJ behind his back. When Cassie asks her mother about this, Mama comments: *'Some folks just like to keep other folks around to laugh at them ... use them.'* She adds that TJ is not 'dumb': *'He just wants attention.'* ✪ How far do you agree?

Mr Jamison arrives with a warning: Thurston Wallace has been saying that he's going to stop the black families taking their business away from his store. ✪ Notice how Mr Jamison respectfully addresses Mama as *Miz Logan*. What does Mr Granger call her? Papa refuses to be dismayed by the bad news and tucks in enthusiastically to the meal of *Good ole butter beans and cornbread.*

A strange phrase, *spring drooped quickly toward summer,* personifies the season changing, and leads into the information that Papa is delaying his return to the railroad because he feels that the trouble with the Wallaces is not over. There is a **foreshadowing** (quite literally!) of events worsening, in the description of Mama speaking *from the deepening shadows*. Moments later Joe Avery and Silas Lanier arrive to say that they've been forced to pull out of shopping at Vicksburg. Granger has increased the amount of cotton they have to give him, and has threatened to evict them. Meanwhile the Wallaces have threatened them with the chain gang (hard labour, in chains) if they cannot pay their debts at the store.

Notice Papa's sudden outburst when he grabs Stacey and reprimands him for criticizing Avery and Lanier. Moments later he forgives Stacey and reassures Cassie, comparing the Logans to a fig tree (p. 166). This is an **analogy**, a kind of extended simile. Read the passage. ✪ Why are the Logans (and families like them) like a fig tree? What is the lesson to be learned from the tree?

Cassie does her usual eavesdropping to tell us about Mama discussing with Papa whether or not he should go to Vicksburg, and whether he should take Stacey (p. 167). ✪ Why does Papa want to take him? During this conversation, Mama snaps at Papa that Stacey has more brains than TJ, and that TJ has *gotten out of hand*. ✪ Papa thinks she's bitter. About what? Do you think she is? Mama comments prophetically that TJ is *headed for a whole lot of trouble*. We see something of the couple's relationship in that Papa still plans to go to Vicksburg, and yet they end the scene laughing and affectionate towards each other.

Papa goes to Vicksburg with Mr Morrison and Stacey. When they are late returning, Mama and Big Ma start to worry, and Cassie is afraid without knowing why. Mildred Taylor handles the suspense expertly. The dogs bark and Mama opens the door *in mad haste*. In a moment the two men, and Stacey, appear out of the night. Papa has a broken leg and a head wound.

While Papa sleeps, Stacey tells the children (and us) what has happened. There was a thunderstorm – which sets up the right atmosphere for stormy events. They lost the wheels off their wagon – probably due to someone tampering with them in Vicksburg. While they were trying to fix the wagon a car appeared out of the darkness and someone shot Papa. Then Stacey was unable to hold the mule still and so the wagon ran over Papa's leg and broke it. Stacey blames himself.

It seems that Mr Morrison has been a hero, ducking into the darkness and then seriously injuring the men with his bare hands. One of them he picks up like a sack of chicken feathers, throwing him down on the ground. Stacey hears bones cracking, cursing and crying.

Notice how Cassie comforts Stacey (p. 173) when he blames himself, and how he in turn comforts Christopher-John and Little Man. The Logan family support each other in times of adversity.

Testing times

? Make a Mind Map or two-column list to show the reasons for and against shopping at Vicksburg for Mr Avery and Mr Lanier.

? Picture the scene in which the Wallaces attack. Jot down key images and sounds you would include if you were filming it. How would you convey the confusion – exaggerated by darkness and rain, the danger, Stacey's fear and Mr Morrison's feat of strength and bravery?

luckily you don't have to be a superhero – give yourself a break!

10 Money worries and a feat of strength

◆ Mama and Papa discuss family finances.
◆ Mr Morrison takes the children on the wagon.
◆ Mr Morrison moves the Wallaces' truck.
◆ Jeremy reports that TJ and the Simms boys are stealing.
◆ The bank wants its money back.
◆ Hammer sells his car to help out.
◆ TJ turns up at the revival hoping to impress.

As with several other chapters, the key theme is broached by an opening line of dialogue: money worries loom large for the Logans. Later on, another brush with the Wallaces brings a showdown closer. Meanwhile TJ is going rapidly downhill.

MONEY WORRIES

Mama and Papa discuss how they will keep up payments on their mortgage. It will be hard. They consider asking Hammer for help, but Papa is reluctant to let his hot-tempered brother know about his broken leg and how he got it. We get an insight into the Logans' lifestyle when they discuss their food necessities (p. 176).

Papa is frustrated by the situation, and by his immobility, and talks about *doing things Hammer's way*. Perhaps it is comforting to him to know that Thurston and Dewberry Wallace have not yet recovered from their injuries either.

MR MORRISON'S BIG FEAT

Unable to find any work, Mr Morrison gets Papa's permission to take a seed-planting tool over to Mr Wiggins. The children go along for the ride. The weather is good, and everything seems fine as they speed happily past the blooming cotton, with Mr Morrison singing in his deep voice and the children – except Stacey – joining in. Then a battered pickup truck appears.

The truck veers to block the road and out steps Kaleb Wallace. He spits out his anger for the injuries the big man gave Thurston and Dewberry in the attack (Ch. 9). He bitterly objects to the fact that Mr Morrison is *still runnin' round free as a white man*. His words say a lot about race relations in Mississippi. ❂ What would you say to him if you were Mr Morrison? Would it help?

Mr Morrison does not try to reason with the enraged man. When it is clear that Kaleb Wallace does not intend to move his truck, Mr Morrison first checks that there is no gun in it. Then, *his muscles flexing tightly against his thin shirt and the sweat popping off his skin like oil on water* (note the simile!), this giant of a man simply lifts the Wallace truck one end at a time, putting it down *as gently as a sleeping child*. Kaleb Wallace is *mute* (speechless).

STYLE AND LANGUAGE

The paragraph beginning *August dawned blue and hot* (pp. 181–2) shows how atmosphere is built up by setting. Here the setting is the Mississippi countryside, and the weather becomes part of it. Notice the image describing the heat, which *swooped low over the land clinging like an invisible shroud* (a shroud clothes a corpse). The people move *as if under water*. The crops are personified as stretching tiredly skyward. ❂ Overall the imagery is effective, but is it overdone or contradictory? Does the image of a swooping shroud work for you?

MESSAGES

The Logan children meet up with Jeremy in the forest. It sounds pleasant to sit there by the pond, with a watermelon chilling. Jeremy acts as a messenger from the white world – as does Mr Jamison. Remember the connection: their names begin with J, which sounds like the *g* in 'messenger'. Jeremy says that TJ and the Simms boys are stealing now. This prepares us for events later in the novel. We also hear about Jeremy's love of tree-houses. ❂ How does this fit his character?

There is more bad news. Mr Granger has persuaded the bank manager to 'call up the note' on the Logans' loan, which means that they have to repay it immediately. This is against the law, but Papa knows there is no point taking it to court.

THE REVIVAL

At the revival – a week-long Church-based festival – we see a happier side of black community life. Read the description of the *feast* at the bottom of p. 187. In this atmosphere of peace and plenty, Hammer appears – walking because he has sold his Packard to help the family pay the bank. As Hammer says, the family is more important than a car.

Hammer comments on how the hot weather makes people *get dissatisfied with life* and *start looking around for someone to take it out on*. (In modern Britain and the United States, too, inner city riots have started in hot weather.) The coming storm, with the sky a strange yellowish colour and the air suffocating, prepares us for the novel's long-awaited climax.

When TJ appears, nattily dressed and accompanied by the Simms boys, he patronizes the Logans and expects them to be pleased to see him and impressed by his white friends. ❂ How does this make you feel about TJ? As the chapter closes, the focus is still on TJ, disappointed and looking *desolately alone*. Cassie almost feels sorry for him. He goes off to Strawberry with the Simms boys, lured by the promise of the *pearl-handled pistol*. The last line is significant: *... TJ turned his back on us and fled across the field*. TJ has also 'turned his back' metaphorically on his black friends, but his 'fleeing' across the field both suggests his present state of mind and foreshadows events in the next chapter.

Develop your thinking

? Imagine yourself in Mr Morrison's position on the road with Kaleb Wallace. You have a minute to convince Wallace that his treatment of the Logans and black people generally is wrong. You could use some of the words and phrases below.

> self-defence   survival   human beings
> co-operation   equal   under the skin
> law of the land   democracy   justice

? Tick boxes in the table opposite to show which descriptions, in your opinion, apply to TJ or Jeremy. A description could apply to one, both or neither.

	Jeremy	TJ	Neither
Doesn't get on with his family	☐	☐	☐
Shy	☐	☐	☐
Tries to make friends outside own race	☐	☐	☐
Hopeful	☐	☐	☐
Dishonest	☐	☐	☐
Respects his father's views	☐	☐	☐
Lonely	☐	☐	☐
Kind-hearted	☐	☐	☐
Dreamer	☐	☐	☐
Stupid	☐	☐	☐

there's a storm brewing; thunder off and get some fresh air!

11 The pearl-handed pistol

◆ Mr Morrison stands guard.
◆ TJ turns up, badly hurt.
◆ He and the Simms brothers have robbed the Barnett store.
◆ The Simms brothers have beaten up TJ for threatening to reveal their guilt.
◆ Stacey and the other children take TJ home.
◆ White men arrive wanting to lynch TJ. The Averys are brutally beaten.
◆ Mr Jamison prevents a lynching, backed by the sheriff – Granger won't allow lynching on his land.

The chapter starts with the defiant blues song which gives the novel its title. It seems that Mr Morrison is singing it as he guards the Logan house, as he does every night. One wonders when he sleeps! Cassie, too, appears to be something of an insomniac – which enables her to report on adult behaviour and conversation.

When Mr Morrison goes to the back of the house, there is a tapping on the porch. Cassie slips out of bed and discovers TJ. Quickly the other children are awake and TJ is in the boys' room revealing the *deep blue-black swelling of his stomach and chest*, and telling the awful story of how he got it. He tells how he went to the Barnett store with RW and Melvin Simms, and found it shut – as they presumably knew it would be. The Simms brothers it seems, persuaded the gullible TJ to break into the store, and insisted that he have *the much-longed-for gun*. The brothers were intent on stealing the store's strong-box.

The Barnetts woke up, RW hit Mr Barnett with an axe and slapped Mrs Barnett so that she fell, hitting her head. The brothers and TJ then fled, leaving the Barnetts for dead.

TJ tells the Logan children how the brothers beat him up badly when he threatened to tell people what happened. Clearly TJ has been used. So desperate is his plight now that he even admits – belatedly – to having got Mrs Logan fired. He pleads with Stacey to help him get home. Cassie does not want Stacey to help. ❂ Do you think he should? It says a lot about Stacey that despite the past, he does help TJ. The other Logan children insist on coming – even Christopher-John because he does not want to be left behind (p. 200).

As they get TJ to his porch, the storm is *creeping closer now, angrily over the forest depths* in anticipation of the human storm about to take place. In moments the children see car headlights. The Logan children hide in the trees and watch, horrified, while the Wallaces and others – including, ironically, RW and Melvin, break into the Avery house demanding TJ. The rest of the family are treated with brutality – the girls are thrown through the open windows. TJ himself receives another beating, despite his parents' desperate attempts to help him. Only the arrival of Mr Jamison prevents a lynching.

There is *an electric tenseness* in the air, and Mr Jamison calmly, courageously stands up for TJ's right to a trial, despite threats from Thurston that he, too, might be lynched as a *nigger lover*. ✪ What would you say to the men if you were Mr Jamison?

The sheriff arrives, but rather than standing for law and order, he simply brings a message that *'Mr Granger ... ain't gonna stand for no hanging on* his *place.'* We can assume that Granger would not object to a lynch-party being held elsewhere.

As thunder crashes and lightning splits the sky, as if whipping up the madness down below, Stacey sends Cassie and the younger boys to fetch Papa.

Check the evidence

? If Mrs Barnett survives, what 'facts' will she report to the sheriff? (See p. 197.) If possible, work with a partner to role-play him interviewing her a few days after the break-in.

? What is wrong with each of these statements? Re-read pp. 201–4 to check.

- The Avery girls jump through the windows.
- TJ gives up the pearl-handled revolver.
- Mr Jamison is the last to arrive at the Avery house.
- Mr Granger turns up with a message from the sheriff.
- Kaleb Wallace plans to shoot TJ, Mr Logan and
- Mr Morrison.

while Cassie and her brothers get home, take a break from the mounting tension

12 Fire!

- ◆ Cassie and her younger brothers tell the adults about TJ.
- ◆ Papa goes to try to stop a lynching.
- ◆ A fire breaks out – the whole community helps put it out.
- ◆ Jeremy brings news of the fire.
- ◆ Cassie and Little Man survey the damage.
- ◆ Stacey explains how the fire stopped the lynching.
- ◆ It emerges that Papa started the fire.
- ◆ The Logans still fear that TJ may die.

This final chapter continues the events of Chapter 11, bringing a kind of uneasy resolution to the horrors of violence and threats of lynching. Events are described from the setting of the Logan home.

Cassie, Christopher-John and Little Man get home and tell their parents what is happening to the Averys, and especially to TJ. Papa takes his shotgun, grimly resolved to stop the lynching in whatever way he can. His unfinished *'Perhaps ...'* (p. 208) hints that there might be another way to stop it.

Shortly after, Big Ma smells smoke: the cotton is on fire. Mama and Big Ma go to fight the fire with sacks and a washtub full of water – there is no fire brigade. The children are sternly warned to stay in the house. Soon they have a visitor – Jeremy Simms, who once again acts as a messenger. He brings news that everyone – black and white – is out fighting the fire. Papa 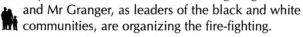 and Mr Granger, as leaders of the black and white communities, are organizing the fire-fighting.

Fortunately it starts to rain heavily, and by dawn the fire is more or less out. Cassie and Little Man go out to see the damage, but Christopher-John for once decides to make his own decision and stay at home – he, too, is growing up.

There is symbolism in what Cassie and Little Man see. The old oak tree – perhaps a symbol of deep family roots – has survived. The figures systematically swatting out the last smoulderings of the fire wear handkerchiefs on their faces to filter the smoke, which obscures their identity. This emphasizes the fact that – for now – black and white are united in a shared emergency.

We hear more of what has happened from Stacey
(pp. 216–17). Mr Jamison did his best to stop the lynching,
but in the end it took the fire to divert attention from TJ, so
that Mr Jamison and the sheriff were able to take him away.

People in the community assume that lighting started the fire,
but Stacey knows otherwise, and Mr Jamison seems to have a
shrewd idea about it too. Soon Cassie realizes: Papa started
the fire, sacrificing a quarter of the Logan cotton crop to save
TJ. We see another important step in Cassie's growing up at the
top of p. 219: *And it came to me that this was one of those*
 known and unknown things, something never to be
spoken, not even to each other.

As the family begin to grieve, the final focus is on Cassie, as
she thinks of TJ. Although she never liked him, the enormity of
what has happened, and the fact that TJ will never be free
again, sinks in, and she weeps ... *for TJ. For TJ and the land.*

The final frontier

? The paragraph starting, *Everything. I poured out everything* (p. 207) summarizes recent events. Read it and quickly Mind Map the things to which it refers.

? Slice up the sweet potato pie chart below to reflect your view of how the following characters share the blame for TJ's downfall: Mrs Logan (who failed him for cheating), Stacey (who blames himself), his parents, RW and Melvin, TJ.

? What will happen next? Will TJ go free, join the chain gang, hang, or escape? Will the Logans keep their land? Make notes for Chapter 1 of your own sequel to *Roll of Thunder.* Then see if great minds really do think alike: read Mildred Taylor's sequel, *Let the Circle be Unbroken.*

while the smoke clears, have a change of scene and a well-earned break

Answers to tests

Getting to know the characters (p. 30)

1 Little Man – he is independent and likes to look smart.
2 Stacey – as the eldest, he has some authority over the others – even Cassie.
3 Papa – he takes time to teach his children what they need to know.
4 TJ – he's a cheat and hopes to get Stacey to co-operate with him.
5 TJ – he likes to tease and make himself feel superior.
6 Cassie – she won't stand for any nonsense, from TJ or anyone else.
7 Cristopher-John – his kind, sensitive nature makes him sympathize with Claude.
8 Stacey – he is beginning to understand the racist world in which he lives, and explains it to his younger brothers and sister.

Education for all (p. 33)

Wordsearch: Miss Crocker – patronizing, stiff, conservative, prim; Mrs Logan – radical, unorthodox, fair, pretty; both – strict, professional, keen, trained.

Boost your learning (p. 35)

1 Big Ma; 2 Stacey; 3 Mama; 4 Papa; 5 Mr Morrison; 6 Papa; 7 Christopher-John; 8 Mr Avery.

What have *you* learned? (p. 47)

1 Stacey; 2 TJ; 3 Barnett; 4 Big Ma; 5 Mr Simms; 6 Jeremy.

Test your recall (p. 52)

(b), (a), (c)
18 (Averys: 8 children + 2 parents; Logans: 4 children + 4 adults)

TOPICS FOR DISCUSSION AND BRAINSTORMING

One of the best ways to revise is with one or more friends. Even if you're with someone who hardly knows the text, having to explain things to your friend will help you to organize your own thoughts and memorize key points. If you're with someone who knows the text, you'll be able to help each other.

Discussion will also help you to develop interesting new ideas that perhaps neither of you would have had alone. Use a brainstorming approach to tackle any of the topics listed below. Allow yourself to share whatever ideas come into your head – however silly they seem. This will get you thinking creatively.

Whether alone or with a friend, use Mind Mapping (see p. vii) to help you brainstorm and organize your ideas. If with a friend, use a large sheet of paper and coloured pens.

Any of the topics below could be set for coursework or feature in an exam paper, but even if you think you've found a similar question, do make sure you plan your answer for the precise question given.

TOPICS

1 How does each of the major child characters develop in the novel?

2 In what ways do the Logans offer a model of the ideal family, and how successful is the author in making them realistic characters at the same time?

3 What injustices in the novel do you feel most strongly about, and why?

4 How does Mildred Taylor portray white characters in the novel, and how do their attitudes to blacks differ?

5 Take three contrasting episodes in the novel, and consider how you would present them (a) in a film, and (b) on stage.

6 What evidence of hope for race relations in Mississippi is there in the novel?

7 How does the author convey what life was like in Mississippi in the 1930s, and how is it relevant to the present day?

8 What role does Mr Morrison play in the Logan family, and in the novel?

*I*n all your study, in coursework, and in exams, be aware of the following:

- **Characterization** – the characters and how we know about them (e.g. what they say and do, how the author describes them), their relationships, and how they develop.
- **Plot and structure** – what happens and how it is organized into parts or episodes.
- **Setting and atmosphere** – the changing physical scene and how it reflects the story (e.g. storms reflecting human violence).
- **Style and language** – the author's choice of words, and literary devices such as imagery, and how these reflect the **mood**.
- **Viewpoint** – how the story is told (e.g. through an imaginary narrator, or in the third person but through the eyes of one character – 'She was furious – how dare he!').
- **Social and historical context** – influences on the author (see 'Background' in this guide).

*D*evelop your ability to:

- Relate **detail** to **broader content, meaning and style**.
- Show understanding of the author's **intentions, technique and meaning** (brief and appropriate comparisons with other works by the same author will gain marks).
- Give **personal response and interpretation**, backed up by **examples** and short **quotations**.
- **Evaluate** the author's achievement. (How far does the author succeed? Give your reasons.)

*M*ake sure you:

- Know how to use **paragraphs** correctly.
- Use a wide range of **vocabulary** and sentence structure.
- Use short, appropriate quotations as **evidence** of your understanding of that part of the text.
- Use the correct **literary terms** to explain how an author achieves effects with language.

THE EXAM ESSAY

Planning

You will probably have about an hour for one essay. It is worth spending about ten minutes planning it. An excellent way to do this is in the three stages below.

1 **Mind Map** your ideas, without worrying about their order yet.
2 **Order** the relevant ideas (the ones that really relate to the question) by numbering them in the order in which you will write the essay.
3 **Gather** your evidence and short quotes.

You could remember this as the **MOG** technique.

Then write the essay, allowing five minutes at the end for checking relevance, and spelling, grammar and punctuation.

REMEMBER!

Stick to the question, and always **back up** your points with evidence in the form of examples and short quotations. Note: you can use '. . .' for unimportant words missed out in a quotation.

Model answer and plan

The next (and final) chapter consists of a model answer to an exam question on *Roll of Thunder, Hear My Cry*, with the Mind Map and essay plan used to write it. Don't be put off if you think you couldn't write an essay like this yet. You'll develop your skills if you work at them. Even if you're reading this the night before the exam, you can easily memorize the MOG technique in order to do your personal best.

The model answer and essay plan are good examples for you to follow, but don't try to learn them off by heart. It's better to pay close attention to the wording of the question you choose to answer in the exam, and allow Mind Mapping to help you think creatively and structurally.

Before reading the answer, you might like to do a plan of your own, then compare it with the example. The numbered points, with comments at the end, show why it's a good answer.

MODEL ANSWER AND ESSAY PLAN

QUESTION

'TJ is an unlikeable boy who has only himself to blame for the situation he gets into at the end of the novel.' How far do you agree?

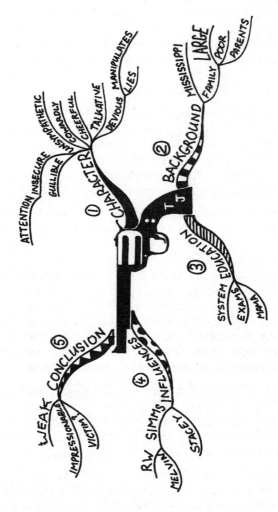

You should consider:

- TJ's character
- his background and education
- the influences on him.

PLAN

1 TJ's character; his good and bad points; his insecurity.
2 Effects of background: big family, loving but weak parents; poverty; racism of Mississippi.
3 Has education failed him? System (repeating years); exams; cheating.
4 Influences: Stacey and the Logans; RW and Melvin Simms.
5 Conclusion: weak, impressionable; to some extent a victim.

ESSAY

TJ is introduced as a cheerful, friendly boy whose jaunty step reflects his happy-go-lucky approach to life. We quickly find, however, that he often wants something out of his friends, and he can be devious in getting it. We see this when he tries to get Stacey to help him cheat in school tests. When this fails, he sneakily tries to find the answers to a test for himself.[1]

TJ does not mind getting others into trouble if it gets him off the hook. Claude suffers a beating because TJ lies to their parents about the Wallace store. Similarly, TJ fails to own up when Mrs Logan finds his 'cheat notes' on Stacey's desk. When Stacey goes to teach him a lesson, even the way he fights is sneaky – pretending to be badly hurt.[2]

In TJ's favour,[3] he is always communicative, but even this has a bad side. He hangs on to his news to get the maximum attention from his audience, teasing the Logan children irritatingly: 'Now, this kind of information ain't for the ears of little kids so I really shouldn't tell y'all –',[4] and boasting about his own intelligence and bravery. When Mrs Logan fails him in his exam he says too much about her to Kaleb Wallace and gets her fired.[5] True to form, he lies about this as well.

The pathetic thing about TJ is that, despite his cockiness, he is insecure and craves attention. As Mrs Logan very significantly tells her daughter, 'TJ's not "dumb" Cassie. He just wants attention, but he's going after it the wrong way.'[6]

He sounds surprised and hurt when Stacey – his only real friend – tells him, 'We don't want no more to do with you.' It is out of desperate neediness that he screams after the Logan children, 'Got me better friends than y'all! They give me things and treat me like I'm a man and ... they white too ...'[7] The way Mildred Taylor describes his voice fading into the wind emphasizes the emptiness of his words and what a pathetic figure he is.[8]

Although TJ has many bad points, he has had a lot of disadvantages to deal with. He is the eldest of eight children, and probably gets little attention from his parents. The family is also very poor. Even on the first day back at school, TJ wears no shoes.[9] We see how difficult TJ finds this poverty when in Chapter 8 he cries, 'All y'all Logans think y'all so doggone much with y'all's new coats and books and shiny new Packards!'[4]

TJ's parents are overburdened and weak, and fail to give him the discipline he needs. Behind this is the problem of racism in Mississippi, which keeps sharecropping families like the Averys in poverty.[10] Mary Logan comments on TJ to her husband, '... the boy's gotten out of hand, and doesn't seem like anybody's doing anything about it.'[6] But the Logans do not do anything about it either.

Mrs Logan 'fails' TJ for cheating in an exam, but TJ's education fails him in a different sense. If he does not pass the year-end exam he will have to return to the same class, with the same teacher for another year. This must be humiliating for TJ. But there is no suggestion that he gets any special help for his 'special needs' from Mrs Logan or anyone else.[11]

When the Logan children turn their backs on him, TJ is thrown onto the Simms brothers, his new-found 'friends'. We know from what David Logan has said to Stacey that this is likely to lead to trouble. For someone manipulative, TJ is remarkably gullible, and he seems to convince himself that the Simms brothers value him: 'Everything I want they give me 'cause they really likes me. I'm they best friend.'[4] His vulnerability is so obvious that even Cassie thinks he looks 'desolately alone' and almost feels sorry for him.

TJ is a fool to be persuaded into helping the Simms boys rob the Barnett store. Perhaps his longing for the pearl-handled pistol blinds him to this - as well as his need to be liked. However, it is hard not to pity him when it all goes wrong and they beat him up, especially when he appeals to the Logans for help, and finally admits to lying about Mrs Logan.[12]

No one could call TJ a really likeable or heroic character.[13] However, he does have a lot of good in him, and he would probably not 'go bad' in different social circumstances, or with more help from the adults around him. Moreover, the Simms boys play on his weakness, and use him. Therefore he is to a large extent a victim – a weak and impressionable boy who deserves help, not lynching.[14]

WHAT'S SO GOOD ABOUT IT?

1 Uses examples to back up a claim.
2 Shows knowledge of detail and ability to interpret the character's action.
3 Good introduction to a more positive trait.
4 Uses a quotation *from* the character to back up a point.
5 Makes a helpful connection between two events.
6 Use of a quotation *about* the character to back up a point well made.
7 Personal interpretation of a key quotation.
8 Awareness of how author's style achieves an effect.
9 Observation and interpretation of a descriptive detail.
10 Shows awareness of social context.
11 Well-argued original interpretation.
12 Personal response.
13 Refers back to the question.
14 Sums up views without repetition.

GLOSSARY OF LITERARY TERMS

alliteration   repetition of a sound at the beginnings of words; e.g. *low over the land.*

analogy   a kind of extended **simile** (see separate entry), explaining one thing in terms of another.

context   the social and historical influences on the author.

first-person narrative   the style of story-telling in which a character speaks directly to the reader: 'I … me … my …'.

foreshadowing   an indirect warning of things to come, often through **imagery**.

image   a word picture used to make an idea come alive; e.g. a **metaphor**, **simile**, or **personification** (see separate entries).

imagery   the kind of word picture used to make an idea come alive.

irony   (1) where the author or a character says the opposite of what he or she really thinks, or pretends ignorance of the true facts, usually for the sake of humour or ridicule; (2) where events turn out in what seems a particularly inappropriate way, as if mocking human effort.

metaphor   a description of a thing as if it were something essentially different but also in some way similar; e.g. *Little Man … saucer-eyed* (Ch. 3).

mood   the overall emotional effect of a passage, created by the author's **imagery** (see separate entry) and choice of words.

personification   a description of a thing as if it were a person; e.g. *the December sun was creeping warily* (Ch. 5).

prose   language in which, unlike verse, there is no set number of syllables in a line, and no rhyming.

setting   the place in which the action occurs, usually affecting the atmosphere; e.g. the forest.

simile   a comparison of two things different in most ways but somehow similar; e.g. the children *skidding like frightened puppies* (Ch. 3).

structure   the overall pattern of the plot.

theme   an idea explored by an author; e.g. race.

viewpoint   how the story is told; e.g. through action, or in discussion between characters. The viewpoint may include a narrator's bias or feelings about events. In *Roll of Thunder* the story is told through Cassie's eyes.

INDEX